Plain Language in Government Writing

A STEP-BY-STEP GUIDE

Plain Language in Government Writing

A STEP-BY-STEP GUIDE

Judith Gillespie Myers, Ph.D.

MANAGEMENTCONCEPTS

MANAGEMENTCONCEPTS
8230 Leesburg Pike, Suite 800
Vienna, VA 22182
(703) 790-9595
Fax: (703) 790-1371
www.managementconcepts.com

Printed in the United States of America

Library of Congress Cataloging-in-Publication Data

Myers, Judith Gillespie, 1942-
Plain language in government writing : a step-by-step guide / Judith Gillespie Myers.
p. cm.
ISBN-13 978-1-56726-224-7
ISBN-10 1-56726-224-4

1. Government report writing—Handbooks, manuals, etc. 2. Government report writing—United States. 3. Authorship—Handbooks, manuals, etc. I. Title.
JF1525.R46M96 2008
808'.066351—dc22

2008001656

10 9 8 7 6 5 4 3 2

About the Author

Judith Gillespie Myers, Ph.D., is an instructor and writer who has taught writing skills to hundreds of students, many of them government employees. Her publications include *Essentials of School Management, Banishing Bureaucratese: Using Plain Language in Government Writing, How to Select and Use Learning Tools,* and *Enhance Learning Retention,* as well as numerous articles and more than 20 training manuals. As a journalist, radio newscaster, and news editor, Dr. Myers has written numerous articles and news items. She received her doctorate from American University in Washington, D.C.

To all the future writers of the world—
including Rory, Mary Kate, Liam, and Paige.

Contents

Foreword

The plain language movement has been around for decades. Fortunately for the average citizen, it seems finally to be getting a foothold in the halls of government—normally a bastion of obscure, convoluted writing. Given a boost by the plain language initiative of Al Gore's National Performance Review, some agencies seem to be making a commitment to communicate more clearly with citizens.

The Veterans Benefits Administration has labored for over ten years to write better letters to veterans. The National Institutes of Health holds a plain language awards ceremony, recognizing over 50 winners from a pool of several hundred nominations of brochures, pamphlets, newsletters, web pages, and other modes of public communication. The Department of the Interior issues many of its new regulations in plain language. The Social Security Administration has clarified some of its most important forms. Even the Internal Revenue Service is getting onboard, trying to clarify some of its notices and forms.

Plain language documents from the public sector, such as insurance policies, loan agreements, and leases, are building public recognition that all official writing does not have to be difficult and obscure. This may create a public demand that further encourages the government to rethink the normal way it communicates with citizens. Congress is starting to take an interest—in 2007, bills were introduced in both the House (Bruce Braley of Iowa) and the Senate (Daniel Akaka of Hawaii) that would require federal agencies to write certain documents in plain language.

Getting the government to write more clearly will not be an easy task. Decades of bureaucrat habits have created a commonly accepted model of government writing that does not recognize clarity as an important principle of communication. Government writers rarely think about the reader's needs, knowledge of the subject matter, and reading skill. And even once a government office makes a commitment to clearer communication, the road is not easy. Clear writing, despite a simple-looking outcome, is tough work. It takes clear thinking about what one is doing, a clear vision of what one wants to communicate, and an understanding of the nature of the audience.

Judy Myers' new book on plain language in government writing is an outstanding tool for government writers who want to accept the challenge of writing more clearly to their customers. Basing much of her discussion on the federal plain language guidelines from www.plainlanguage.gov, Dr. Myers expands on the principles in those guidelines and provides a wealth of advice that will make your writing task easier. The many before-and-after examples taken from that website clarify the principles she presents and are directly relevant to government writing. You can get sound, practical advice on an amazing number of document types, from letters and white papers to meeting minutes, trip reports, help files, and abstracts. I wish her advice on writing letters of recommendation was available during my government career; that was one of the tasks I dreaded the most.

Read Dr. Myer's discussion of writing principles, and consult her discussions of document types whenever you take on a writing task. The American public will be glad you did.

Dr. Annetta L. Cheek
Falls Church, VA

Preface

In this day of bursting email boxes and an ever-expanding blogosphere, effective writing skills are more important than ever. To capture the attention of your reader and convey a concise, clear message is a daunting challenge. Yet communication is the *sine qua non* of the business world and an indispensable skill for all employees. Whether you are writing a 30-page report or a one-paragraph email, what and how you write affects how people interpret and respond to your message.

If you write on behalf of a government agency, your communication must be clear and understandable, especially when you are telling people how to obtain benefits or comply with requirements. Traditionally, government documents were written in legalistic, confusing language. Too often, this style resulted in reader frustration, lawsuits, and lack of trust between citizens and their government.

Today, those in both government and industry are appreciating the value of plain, understandable English. One group, the Plain Language Action and Information Network (PLAIN), is at the center of the movement to spread the use of plain language in the United States. Its website, www.plainlanguage.gov, was created to help all writers learn about and use plain language.

This book was inspired by that website and builds upon the concepts and tools presented in *Banishing Bureaucratese: Using Plain Language in Government Writing*, published in 2001. *Plain Language in Government Writing: A Step-by-Step Guide* expands upon the earlier book and strives to use the guidance from PLAIN to offer a practical tool for writers in an easy-to-follow guide. By learning the stages of writing and how to execute each stage, you can make writing easier and more enjoyable.

This book is designed to help you:

- Write in reader-friendly, plain language
- Gain confidence in your ability to get the results you want when you write
- Recognize good writing and identify what makes it good
- Learn techniques that make writing better and easier to do

- Form good writing habits through structured practice, with immediate feedback

- Diagnose your writing skills to identify areas needing improvement

- Formulate plans to continue your development

These improved skills will help you become more effective in your business writing and in your personal writing as well.

When we use the term "business writing," we are referring to documents produced in the line of work, regardless of the specific workplace setting. Thus, memos, letters, and reports sent out by a government agency are as much business writing as those sent out by a corporation or a non-profit association. Although the guidelines presented in this book will help you with any kind of writing, including personal letters, the main focus on the book is on business, or workplace, writing.

Good writing skills are in demand by employers. The ability to write well correlates highly with the ability to think well—to analyze information, weigh alternatives, and make decisions. No one gets to the top without being able to write well.

Because writing is the process of getting thoughts onto paper, clear writing helps the writer develop, focus, and organize ideas. It helps writers understand their thoughts better.

So organize your thoughts, write them clearly, present them effectively, and you're well on your way to success in the workplace.

Judith Gillespie Myers
April 2008

Please note that an instructor's guide is available for text adopters. For more information, please contact Management Concepts at pubsupport@managementconcepts.com.

Acknowledgments

I would like to thank everyone on the Management Concepts team who made this publication possible. The help and encouragement provided by Myra Strauss and the hard work and careful editing by Courtney Chiaparas were especially appreciated.

Without the foundation laid by the Plain Language Action and Information Network, this book would not exist in its present form. I am grateful to all the people who established the Network and have kept it going.

And I am deeply grateful for the support and patience of my husband, Geof.

PART I

Process and Stages of Plain Language Writing

CHAPTER 1

Succeeding as a Writer in Today's Workplace

◆ **Mixed Feelings** ◆

Maria had been called into the office of Lee, her supervisor.

"Maria, we're going to give you a promotion. Congratulations!"

"Thank you," said Maria, hardly able to contain her surprise.

"There's one thing you need to know about this promotion," said Lee. "It entails much more writing. I need you to edit the newsletter and send out monthly reports to the budget office. I'd also like weekly updates on the customer service project."

Maria had mixed feelings about her promotion. On the one hand, she was happy about the increase in salary and responsibility. On the other hand, she was a bit worried about the prospect of writing. Maria had not done much writing in her job lately. "I guess I'd better brush up on my business writing skills," she said to herself.

To succeed in the workplace, whether you are in government or elsewhere, you must be able to express yourself effectively, clearly, and persuasively. You must create documents that your readers will read and understand, documents that result in decisions, documents that affect your readers as you intend. Each letter, report, or email that you send out is a reflection on your organization. And it is a reflection on you.

Like Maria, you might find the whole process of writing daunting. Many of us do. And yet, with the right guidance and practice, we can all become better, more effective writers.

COMMON MYTHS ABOUT BUSINESS WRITING

One reason that many people dread writing is that certain myths have become associated with business writing and with the writing process. Do these sound familiar?

1. **Myth 1:** The first rule of business writing is to be businesslike, so a business letter has to sound somewhat unnatural.

   Reality: Business letters should sound natural but professional. While the tone of your letter depends on the context, purpose, and audience, you want to sound friendly and sometimes even informal. The increased use of email has led to more informality in correspondence, so today's letters are typically more conversational than those of the past.

2. **Myth 2:** To convey important government information, your document must sound intellectual and sophisticated.

   Reality: Your primary goal in conveying any information is to make sure the reader understands what you're writing. To achieve this goal, you need to write simply and directly. Law school professor and plain language advocate Joseph Kimble refutes the notion that plain language will "dumb down" important government communication: "Any second-rate writer can make things more complicated; only the best minds and the best writers can cut through. It takes skill and hard work to write in plain language."[1]

3. **Myth 3:** Plain language can't be used for technical writing because technical writing involves complex subjects and uses technical terms.

   Reality: Technical information must be clear and straightforward so that people can understand it, regardless of their technical background. In fact, focus-group results show that even technical experts do not always understand technical language easily or quickly. Using plain language, you can explain technical terms and complex ideas in a way that most readers will understand.

4. **Myth 4:** Really good writers write it right the first time, without revising their drafts.

   Reality: Very few people can write a polished paragraph on the first try. Good writing involves many rewrites and might include complete reorganization. Even after an experienced writer has worked on a manuscript, it goes to a professional editor for revision and polishing before it is published.

   F. Scott Fitzgerald revised his stories at least five times before they were published. Ernest Hemingway once told a reporter that he wrote the ending to *A Farewell to Arms* 39 times before he was satisfied. When asked what it was that stumped him, Hemingway responded, "Getting the words right." Vladimir Nabokov once admitted that he rewrote every word he had ever published and wore out his erasers before his pencils.

5. **Myth 5:** Grammar and punctuation are the most important aspects of learning to write well.

   Reality: The most important point is to communicate your message clearly. If the reader doesn't understand what you're saying, why bother to write? However, having an error in grammar or punctuation is like walking out of the house in your best formal attire with a ketchup stain on your shirt: It detracts from the message.

6. **Myth 6:** You need to keep control of your writing. This means correcting each idea as it comes to you, before you put it down on paper.

   Reality: As soon as your ideas start to flow, you should begin writing so you won't lose them; you can always go back later and make minor modifications. As we will discuss later, it's important to divide writing into stages and not to mix the stages. In the drafting stage, you want to capture those first thoughts, not censor them.

   Natalie Goldberg describes first thoughts this way:

   > *First thoughts have tremendous energy. It is the way the mind first flashes on something. The internal censor usually squelches them, so we live in the realm of second and third thoughts, thoughts on thought, twice and three times removed from the direct connection of the first fresh flash . . . . First thoughts are also unencumbered by ego, by that mechanism in us that tries to be in control. . . .*[2]

7. **Myth 7:** You should strive for long sentences and long words in business documents.

Reality: A document with long sentences and many syllables is considered more difficult to read than one with shorter sentences and fewer syllables. For most business writing, the ideal sentence length is 15 to 20 words, or about an eighth- or ninth-grade reading level.

The guidelines at www.plainlanguage.gov give the reasons for short sentences:

> *Sentences loaded with dependent clauses and exceptions confuse the reader by losing the main point in a forest of words. Resist the temptation to put everything in one sentence; break up your idea into its parts and make each one the subject of its own sentence.*[3]

8. **Myth 8:** A document is a document. Once you learn how to write, you can use the same design and style from one workplace to the next.

   Reality: You need to consider your organization's culture. Consider, for example, the difference between an office in the U.S. Department of Defense that deals with top-secret information and an office in a county recreation department that staffs local parks. The recreation department probably would have a much more informal environment, and that informality would be reflected in its documents.

   The style of documents you write also depends on the mission of your organization and the mission of your specific office. A letter from the Office of the Under Secretary of Defense for Personnel and Readiness to a prospective employee would differ dramatically from a letter to the Secretary of Defense for Intelligence Oversight describing lapses in intelligence in an Army installation. Noting the conventions, practices, and mission of your organization will help you compose appropriate, professional documents.

9. **Myth 9:** Templates should never be used for workplace communication.

   Reality: Templates, or boilerplate forms, are useful for routine correspondence. They save time because the writer does not have to recreate the formatting for every communication. They also provide direction to writers about which information is critical. Because they include headings and subheadings, they reduce wordiness and help readers find the information they need. However, although most offices use these form letters for routine correspondence, serious communication rarely fits into such forms. Such issues require careful consideration of purpose, audience, context, and message.

10. **Myth 10:** Not everyone in the workplace needs to be concerned about writing.

Reality: In today's professional environment, all employees should know how to compose their own correspondence, reports, and, of course, email. Even if you don't do much writing now, you need to prepare yourself for additional responsibilities or a job change. If you have assistants to write routine correspondence, you must approve such documents before they go out. And you must compose letters or reports for any nonroutine or complex situations.

THE IMPORTANCE OF PLAIN LANGUAGE IN GOVERNMENT WRITING

You can reduce confusion or misinterpretation in all your writing while still giving readers the technical information they need. The best way to do this is to:

- Engage your readers
- Write clearly and concisely
- Put the main idea first
- Write in a visually appealing style

Government writing presents a special challenge. Government documents often contain technical information, and they go out to multiple audiences—some highly knowledgeable, some less so.

Government documents have traditionally contained gobbledygook—jargon and complicated, legalistic language. These uninviting letters and reports sound like they are addressed to technical experts and lawyers rather than to readers who need to be influenced or informed.

Presidential Efforts to Improve Government Writing

For decades, presidents and political leaders have urged clear writing in government documents. James Madison wrote in 1788, "It will be of little avail to the people, that the laws are made by men of their own choice, if the laws be so voluminous that they cannot be read, or so incoherent that they cannot be understood."[4]

Franklin Roosevelt cringed at the convoluted wording of the following blackout order during World War II:

> *Such preparations shall be made as will completely obscure all Federal buildings and non-Federal buildings occupied by the government during an air raid for any period of time from visibility by reason of internal or external illumination.*[5]

"Tell them," Roosevelt said, "that in buildings where they have to keep the work going to put something across the windows."[6]

In an attempt to cut the government gobbledygook, President Nixon ordered that the *Federal Register* be written in "layman's terms." President Carter signed an executive order directing that federal regulations be "easy to understand by those who are required to comply with them." A few federal agencies responded by publishing regulations that were more clearly written, although the efforts were sporadic.

The most recent program to improve government writing was President Clinton's 1998 directive requiring agencies to use plain English. Vice President Gore issued guidance on how to implement the directive. Then several agencies set up what is now called PLAIN—the Plain Language Action and Information Network, a government-wide group to improve communications from the federal government to the public.[7] Each agency had a plain language official, and the government rewarded agencies that made significant improvements in their documents. The PLAIN website—www.plainlanguage.gov—contains numerous resources to help writers communicate more clearly.

In 1993 President Clinton issued Executive Order 12866, ordering that agencies draft their regulations "to be simple and easy to understand, with the goal of minimizing the potential for uncertainty." It also required that information provided to the public be in "plain, understandable language."[8]

President Clinton's memorandum of June 1, 1998, on this topic stated:

> *Plain language documents have logical organization, easy-to-read design features; common, everyday words, except for necessary technical terms; 'you' and other pronouns; the active voice; and short sentences.*[9]

Although the Bush Administration did not have a formal plain language initiative, it did require agencies to follow the requirements in Executive Order 12866, which includes the use of plain language. Nevertheless, the use of bureaucratese—or bureaucratic language—continued.

Other Plain Language Programs

Efforts to eliminate bureaucratese have not come from the White House alone. Many federal agencies, state government entities, and other organizations have initiated programs to enforce plain language.

Many states have laws requiring that consumer statutes be written in plain language. The Federal Judicial Center in Washington, D.C., teaches federal judges to write their opinions in plain English.

- The U.S. Securities and Exchange Commission has drafted a plain English handbook.

- The Office of Management and Budget has issued government-wide guidance establishing a standard format for grant announcements.

- The National Institutes of Health's Plain Language Initiative requires plain language in all new documents written for the public, other government entities, and fellow workers.

- The American Bar Association has issued the following resolution encouraging agencies to write regulations in plain language:[10]

RESOLVED, *That the American Bar Association urges agencies to use plain language in writing regulations, as a means of promoting the understanding of legal obligations, using such techniques as:*

- *Organizing them for the convenience of their readers;*
- *Using direct and easily understood language;*
- *Writing in short sentences, in the active voice; and*
- *Using helpful stylistic devices, such as question-and-answer formats, vertical lists, spacing that facilitates clarity, and tables.*

To avoid problems in the use of plain language techniques, agencies should:

- *Take into account possible judicial interpretations as well as user understanding;*
- *Clearly state the obligations and rights of persons affected, as well as those of the agency; and*

- *Identify and explain all intended changes when revising regulations.*

- The Department of the Interior issues many of its new regulations in plain language. Some good examples are the Bureau of Indian Affairs' Housing Improvement Program and the Mineral Management Service's rules on relief or reduction of royalty rates.

- The Federal Aviation Administration issued an internal directive requiring staff to write in plain language.

- The Office of the Federal Register is revising its requirements and allowing many plain language tools and techniques. It has produced two excellent aids for using plain language, *Making Regulations Readable* and *Drafting Legal Documents*.

- The Food and Drug Administration realizes that low health literacy, combined with the increasing incidence of chronic health problems like diabetes and obesity, results in serious public health problems. To fight these problems most effectively, FDA knows it is more important than ever to use plain language so consumers get information that is clear, informative, and effective in helping them improve or maintain their health.

- The Veteran's Benefits Administration has trained many thousands of staff in reader-focused writing, so that letters and notices to veterans are easier to read and veterans understand better how to apply for the benefits they deserve.

- The Department of Health and Human Services issued a guide for writing Health Insurance Portability and Accountability Act (HIPAA) privacy notices in plain language.

- The Securities and Exchange Commission has published a handbook on how to create clear financial-disclosure documents.

- The National Labor Relations Board (NLRB) has issued a revised edition of its style manual, first published in 1983. *The NLRB Style Manual: A Guide for Legal Writing in Plain English* gives guidelines for writing briefs and other documents submitted to the Board and to the Division of Judges.

WHY USE PLAIN LANGUAGE?

Proponents assert that writing documents by using plain language techniques is effective in a number of ways: It saves money, helps prevent lawsuits, pleases readers, and makes your job easier.

Plain Language Saves Money

Joseph Kimble cites a 1991 study showing that writing memos in plain language instead of bureaucratese could save the U.S. Navy $250 million to $350 million a year. Naval officers were given business memos to read. Some memos were written in plain style and some in bureaucratic style. It took officers 17-to-23 percent less time to read the plain memo. Based on the average hourly pay for all naval personnel, the researchers calculated the yearly savings.[11]

As part of a writing project, the Veterans Administration tracked the savings from rewriting just one form letter in plain language. Kimble reports that in one year, one regional VA call center saw the number of calls drop from about 1,100 to about 200. Based on the savings on this letter alone, a VA project coordinator estimated that, if this letter were adopted at VA offices nationwide, the VA would save more than $40,000 a year. And the VA sends out thousands of different letters.[12]

Agencies have been cutting down on administrative costs, too. In the 1970s the Federal Communications Commission rewrote the regulations for CB radios in plain English. The number of calls from people confused by the rules dropped so dramatically that the agency was able to reassign all five people who had been fielding questions full-time.[13]

Examples of how using fewer words has resulted in reduced time and cost—and greater ease of public use—abound throughout the government. One outstanding example is Jane Virga of the Farm Credit Administration, who revised a document explaining the Freedom of Information Act fees. By the time she finished, the size of the document had shrunk from 7,850 to 4,018 words. The revised document's reduced size made it more user-friendly for the public and reduced the printing cost. And, amazingly, the revised document contained more information than the original.[14]

Plain Language Helps Avoid Lawsuits

As an article in *The Editorial Eye* by Mark R. Miller points out, unclear writing is more than annoying. Some courts have called it unconstitutional. He notes the following:

> *A few years ago, the Immigration and Naturalization Service (INS) was taken to court by several aliens the INS had attempted to deport after they had failed to request hearings in document fraud cases. The INS had notified them of their right to request a hearing and informed them that, if they waived that right, they most likely would be deported.*
>
> *The problem? The forms the INS used for notification were so unclear that the aliens didn't understand their rights or the possible legal consequences. The court*

not only ordered INS to rewrite the forms but also prevented the agency from deporting any alien who had received the forms.[15]

Plain Language Pleases Readers

Research shows that readers prefer documents written in plain language and understand them better. For example, Martin Cutts, research director of the Plain Language Commission in the United Kingdom, used his own guidelines to revise a document and later tested it against the original. The result was that 87 percent of the law students tested preferred the revised document. More importantly, when asked a set of 12 questions about either the original or the revised document, students using the revised version performed better on nine out of 12 questions.[16]

Joseph Kimble conducted a similar study by sending two separate surveys to judges and lawyers using paragraphs written in traditional legalese and in plain English, though they were not labeled as such. The readers rated the passages in legalese to be substantially weaker and less persuasive than the versions written in plain English.[17]

Plain Language Makes Your Job Easier

If people understand your documents the first time they read them, they will be less likely to ask for clarification and will be more likely to respond favorably to your message. In addition, clear writing can boost your reputation and enhance your career.

TEST YOURSELF

SELF-ASSESSMENT

The following statements express feelings that many people have about their writing problems. Do you share these feelings? How strongly? For each statement, indicate:

1. Always or almost always
2. Frequently
3. Sometimes
4. Seldom
5. Very rarely or never

In the column on the right, you will find the section of this book that deals with each of these issues.

Your Score	Statement	Chapter(s)
	I have trouble getting started.	Chapter 2
	I have trouble organizing my ideas.	Chapter 2
	I probably say too much.	Chapters 3 and 5
	I probably say too little.	Chapter 5
	People have to follow up to ask me, "What did you mean by that?"	Chapter 5
	My writing sounds forced, unnatural, and not like me.	Chapter 4
	I'm unsure about how formal or businesslike I should be.	Chapter 4

Your Score	Statement	Chapter(s)
	I doubt that what I write is grammatically correct.	Chapter 7
	My attempts to revise my writing don't seem to improve it much.	Chapter 7
	I spend too much time writing for the results I get.	Chapters 2 and 3
	My documents do not seem to look visually appealing.	Chapter 6
	I'm uncomfortable sending email, because I don't know how to express myself well.	Chapter 8
	I don't know how to organize a letter, or how to get started.	Chapter 9
	Writing reports is difficult for me.	Chapter 10
	People don't seem to understand my technical writing.	Chapter 11
	I don't know how to prepare an effective presentation.	Chapter 12
	When working on a group writing project, I'm never certain about my responsibilities.	Chapter 12

If you face workplace writing tasks with dread and fear, you're not alone. Many people share these feelings. Because of common misconceptions, many of us take the wrong approach to writing. We need to learn how to divide the writing process into stages, adapt our writing to fit the workplace, and produce more reader-friendly documents.

The government setting presents some unique challenges to writers because of both the audience and the type of information government entities typically convey. Federal employees are beginning to understand that the plain language initiative isn't simply the federal government's newest writing fad. It saves dollars, keeps writers out of court, makes readers happier, and makes our jobs easier. The cry for clearer writing has been around for a long time. In today's world of information overload, that cry is being heeded.

NOTES

1 Joseph Kimble, "Testifying to Plain Language," testimony before the House Subcommittee on Regulatory Affairs, March 1, 2006, *Michigan Bar Journal* (June 2006), 45.
2 Natalie Goldberg, *Writing Down the Bones: Freeing the Writer Within* (Boston: Shambhala Publications, 1986), 9.
3 Plain Language Action and Information Network, "Break Your Material Into Short Sentences." Online at http://www.plainlanguage.gov (accessed May 5, 2007).
4 James Madison, *The Federalist Papers*, no. 62 (New Rochelle, NY: Arlington House, 1966).
5 Cited in William Zinsser, *On Writing Well: The Classic Guide to Writing Nonfiction*, 7th ed. (New York: HarperCollins, 2006), 7.
6 Ibid.
7 For more information on the history of PLAIN, see "History of Plain Language in the United States." Online at www.plainlanguage.gov (accessed January 2008).
8 President William J. Clinton, "Executive Order 12866 of September 30, 1993: Regulatory Planning and Review," *Federal Register* 58, no. 190 (October 4, 1993). Online at www.archives.gov/federal-register/executive-orders/pdf/12866.pdf (accessed January 2008).

9 President William J. Clinton, memorandum "Plain Language in Government Writing," 1 June 1998. Online at http://govinfo.library.unt.edu/NPR/library/direct/memos/memoeng.html (accessed May 2007).
10 Plain Language Action and Information Network, "American Bar Association Adoption by the House of Delegates." Online at www.plainlanguage.gov (accessed January 2008).
11 Joseph Kimble, "Writing for Dollars, Writing to Please," *The Scribes Journal of Legal Writing* 6 (1996).
12 Ibid.
13 Ibid.
14 Archive, National Partnership for Reinventing Government, "Morley Winograd Plain Language Award Presentations," Washington, D.C., April 6, 2000. Online at http://govinfo.library.unt.edu/npr/library/speeches/040600.html (accessed January 10, 2008).
15 Mark R. Miller, "Is It Plain English Yet? Bureaucratese Makes People Read Between the Lines," *The Editorial Eye* (March 1999).
16 Martin Cutts, "Unspeakable Acts Revisited," *Information Design Journal* 9, no. 1 (1998): 39–43. Cited in Beth Mazur, "Revisiting Plain Language," www.plainlanguage.gov (accessed January 2008).
17 Joseph Kimble, "Writing for Dollars, Writing to Please," *The Scribes Journal of Legal Writing* 6 (1996).

CHAPTER 2

Getting Started: The Planning Stage

◆ **Battling Writer's Block** ◆

In the middle of an extremely busy week, Tom was asked to provide a letter of recommendation for a former employee, Marcia, for admission to engineering school.

Tom sat at his computer and stared at the screen. No ideas came to mind. His mind wandered, and he thought about the things he had to accomplish before the weekend. He was distracted by a conversation outside in the hall. He stared again at the screen and gritted his teeth. Then he remembered what he needed to do—gather information and prepare an outline.

Before planning the letter, Tom collected the data he needed. He reread the instructions from the engineering school to determine exactly what he had been asked to do. He located a copy of Marcia's resume and a brief biography that had appeared in the agency newsletter. Then he talked to some people who had worked with Marcia to find out more about her specific knowledge, skills, and abilities, as well as her work habits and her ways of interacting with coworkers. Finally, he called Marcia and asked her about her purpose for attending engineering school and her plans for the future. He asked Marcia to fax him the personal statement she had written for the application.

Tom then went to lunch and spent the hour thinking about what he wanted to say in the letter. He reflected on Marcia's outstanding qualities. Then he thought about what an engineering school admission officer would want to know.

After Tom returned to his desk, he made the following informal outline:

Recommendation for Marcia Thompson

- First-hand knowledge of Marcia
  - Worked with her for three years
  - Collaborated on many projects
  - Supervised specific project: inspection of bridges
- Personal observations of Marcia's competence handling the XYZ Project
- Hallmark of her character: honesty
- Teammates' observations of Marcia's interpersonal skills and work habits
- Marcia's thoroughness and adherence to quality

- Comments from customers regarding Marcia's abilities and responsiveness
- Reasons why Marcia could benefit from engineering school
- Contributions Marcia could make to engineering school

All of us have felt the way Tom did as he faced his writing task. Whether writing a long report or a memo, we find ourselves staring at a blank screen, our minds wandering. At those times, the writing process can seem so overwhelming that we'd do anything to avoid putting down that first word.

If you're having a difficult time getting started and think you might be experiencing writer's block, try the following:

- *Avoid leaving your project until the last minute.* You'll need time to prepare, plan, write, get away from your project, and edit it.

- *When scheduling your project, give yourself some time to warm up to the topic.* Let your mind wander. Many of your best ideas will occur to you at odd moments during the day or night. But try to set a time limit for this step.

- *Jot down every idea that comes to you, quickly and randomly.* If you find it easier, discuss your project with a colleague or talk into a tape recorder. You can dictate much faster—some say six times faster—than you can write.

- *If you run into a roadblock after you get started, take a break and let your ideas incubate.* When you return in a few minutes or hours, you can select the essential ideas, add new ideas, and delete irrelevant ideas.

- *Don't confuse writing with editing.* Writing proceeds much more easily when writers understand the phases of the writing process:

  – Planning

  – Drafting

  – Editing

Although you might move back and forth from one stage to another, the important thing to remember is not to combine the stages. Each stage requires a distinctly different process and way of thinking. For example, during the drafting phase, you should not edit. Drafting requires that you allow your thoughts to flow freely. If you try to edit while you draft, you'll inhibit the flow of ideas.

GUIDELINES FOR PLANNING

It pays to take the time to plan ahead before you begin writing, even when your message is short and even when you have to write under deadline pressure. It's like looking at a road map before you start driving to a new destination: If you know where you're going before you start, you're less likely to get lost along the way.

For any kind of writing—for emails, letters, or reports—you need to make sure that you understand three things: (1) your purpose, (2) your audience, and (3) your subject.

Know Your Purpose

Before you begin, ask yourself why you are writing. This will save time for both you and others. If you are carrying out an assigned writing project, get as much guidance as possible before you begin. You don't want to spend days or even weeks on a document only to find out that you are on the wrong track.

If this is *not* an assigned writing project, ask yourself the following questions before you start:

- Should *I* be writing this? At this time?
- Would a phone call or meeting be more effective?
- Am I too late to send this?

- Is someone else communicating the same information? Should I check with that person?
- Should I include deadlines? What actions, if any, should I request?
- Should I send this by email, traditional mail, or fax?

Decide what effect you want to have on your reader. Identify the most important idea—the one you want the reader to remember. A one- or two-sentence purpose statement helps get you started. It forces you to decide exactly *why* you are writing. It directs your effort and becomes the lens through which you view the entire writing project. Your purpose statement becomes the lead-in to your outline and often becomes the first words in the document itself.

When writing your purpose statement, ask yourself:

- What's the best outcome for my agency? What do I need to say to get this outcome?
- What's the best outcome for the reader? What do I need to say to get this outcome?

The following are examples of purpose statements:

- To persuade the deputy to add three new staff members to the human resources team

- To provide background information on a policy that is coming up for review

- To direct employees to use a new timesheet procedure

When you don't have a clear and explicit purpose, you run the risk of writing more than is necessary, giving the wrong information, or sending an unclear message.

Know Your Audience

The PLAIN website gives the following advice:

> *You have to grab your reader's attention if you want to get your ideas across. Let's face it, readers want to know just what applies to them. The best way to grab and hold their attention is to figure out who they are and what they want to know. Put yourself in their shoes; it will give you a new perspective.*[1]

Role of the Reader

To determine your reader's technical expertise, you need to consider his or her *role.* For example, a network engineer has different responsibilities, and a different type of expertise, than a personnel manager. Typically, the role of your reader determines what the reader knows about your subject, the reader's decision-making level, and the type or form of information needed.

Your reader's technical expertise will in turn tell you what kind of background information you must supply to guide your reader from Point A to Point B in as straight a line as possible. Also, your reader's knowledge of your subject will determine what kind of technical jargon and acronyms would be appropriate or inappropriate.

Figure 2-1 illustrates the categories of readers, their decision-making levels, their knowledge of the subject, and the type or form of information they need. Although this chart applies to readers of technical information, it is also a useful guide for other types of information.

Likely Reaction of the Reader

Regardless of your reader's role, you need to determine how he or she will react to your document. Are you delivering good news or bad news? Will the reader like your recommendations or resist them? Should you state your case forcefully, or will that make the reader defensive? To gauge your reader's reaction, ask yourself the following questions:

- Is your message in alignment with your reader's goals and values?
- Are you disputing the data?
- Will your reader lose face by accepting your recommendations?

Figure 2-1 ◆ Categories of Readers

Categories of Readers	Managers	Experts or advisors (engineers, accountants)	Operators (field technicians, office workers, salespersons)	General readers ("laypersons")
Decision-Making Level	High level. Will translate your document into action.	Medium level. Analyze information and may influence decision-makers.	Low level. Receive information and adjust jobs accordingly.	Typically low.
Knowledge of Subject	Typically have general understanding but are removed from hands-on detail.	Understand technical aspects of the subject that apply to them.	Understand technical aspects of subject that apply to them.	Usually have least amount of information on the topic.
Type/Form of Information Needed	Brief summaries, background information—the big picture.	Technical details, tables and charts, and appendices of supporting information.	Clear organization, well-written instructions, clarity about how document affects their job.	Definitions of technical terms, frequent graphs, clear statements about how the document affects them.

- Will your message create more work for your reader?
- Will your reader get pressure from his or her manager because of your message?

Once you have answered these questions, you can write your document in a way that minimizes negative reactions.

Writing Regulations for More Than One Reader

A document often has many readers. You might be writing to exporters and importers, coal miners and surface owners, or airlines and passengers. Even if your document goes to only one person, others might read it later. When you write to multiple readers who have a similar knowledge of, and attitude toward, your subject, you can write to one representative person in the audience.

But what if your intended readers have different levels of knowledge or interest or different roles? What do you do? The following are some tips for writing regulations for diverse audiences:[2]

- Break your document down into the essential elements.
- Determine which elements apply to each part of your audience.

- Group the elements according to the audience that will be affected. If you are writing about research grants for university professors, first tell the professors what they have to do and then tell the university accounting department what it has to do.

- Clearly identify to whom you are speaking in each section. Don't make a reader go through material only to find out at the end that the section doesn't apply.

Writing Letters and Reports for More Than One Reader

When you are writing a letter, you generally write to only one person. However, you must consider the possibility of additional readers. For example, if you write to a member of Congress about a constituent problem, someone in the congressperson's office might attach a cover letter and send your letter on to the constituent without any further explanation. Therefore, you must write so that both audiences understand your letter.

Distinguish between primary readers (such as the member of Congress) and secondary readers (such as the constituent). *Primary readers* are those who have the greatest need to know. They are the decision-makers, the ones who will need to act after reading your report. Therefore, they are the ones you should cater to. *Secondary readers* are those who, though interested, do not need the same level of detail.

For reports, consider including the following for both primary and secondary readers:[3]

- A cover memo providing background information and guidance
- An executive summary of your report
- A table of contents
- Informative headings
- Marginal notations
- Definitions of any technical terms
- Appendices or attachments for information of interest only to specialists

TEST YOURSELF

WHO IS THE AUDIENCE?

Below are three versions of the same message, each written for a different audience. Read each version and describe the intended audience. How much knowledge of the topic do you think each audience has? Can you guess the role of each reader? See the Appendix for answers.

1. We modified the M.T.I. by installing a K-59 double-decade circuit. This brightened moving targets by 12 percent and reduced ground clutter by 23 percent.
2. We modified the radar set's Moving Target indicator by installing a special circuit known as the K-59. This increased the brightness of responses from aircraft and decreased returns from fixed objects on the ground.
3. We have modified the airfield radar system to improve its performance. This modification has helped us to differentiate more clearly between low-lying aircraft and high objects on the ground.

Know Your Subject

Once you've determined your purpose and identified your audience, you need to research your subject. Collect all the information you need (but don't overdo it).

- Review:
  - Correspondence
  - Policy directives
  - Administrative memos or any other papers related to your task
- Consult with people who can lend knowledge or insight.
- Analyze your notes or your data collection.

- Digest the material.
- Sift through it to determine what is useful and what is not.
- Organize useful material into meaningful groups.

GUIDELINES FOR BRAINSTORMING AND ORGANIZING

Once you've determined your purpose, audience, and subject, think about what you have to say and then organize your thoughts. The larger your writing project, the more you need to plan and prepare a useful outline. First, spend some time brainstorming. Let your ideas flow freely, get them down on paper, then evaluate and organize them. The following are some suggestions for brainstorming or generating ideas.

The Mind Map

Mind mapping, a technique originated by Tony Buzan, uses a nonlinear, pictorial way of presenting ideas and their relationship to each other.[4] To brainstorm in this way, follow these steps:

- In the center of a large piece of paper, write the most important word or phrase describing your main idea (e.g., a proposal for new software). Circle it.

- Draw lines radiating outward from that main idea. Each line represents another important concept you want to present (e.g., costs).

- Along each line, draw smaller lines representing related or supporting ideas (e.g., software).

- Continue this process, throwing in ideas as they occur to you, until you have developed a wheel-like picture (as shown in Figure 2-2) of the ideas you want to cover.

- Edit your mind map. Think about the relationship of outside items to the center item. Combine or move ideas for better organization.

- Organize those ideas into a traditional outline.

The Questioning Technique

Create an imaginary dialogue in which you play two parts: the writer and the reader. List questions the reader will ask, and write your answers underneath. Answer your questions as clearly and completely as possible. Then organize those ideas into a traditional outline.

Figure 2-2 ◆ The Mind Map

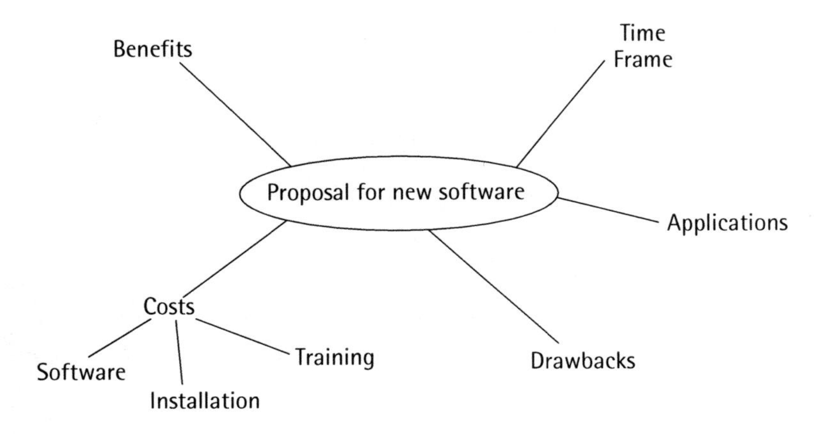

The following are some examples:

Making a presentation:

1. What is this about?
2. Why should I pay attention to it?
3. What's the objective?
4. How will the objective be achieved?
5. How much will it cost?
6. How long will it take?
7. What are the risks?
8. What's the potential payoff?
9. What's the next step?

Conveying information:
1. What's this about?
2. What does it mean to me?
3. What are the details?
4. Which parts are most important?
5. What am I supposed to do about it?
6. How do I start?

Making an interim report:
1. What's this about?
2. Is the project on track?
3. What problems is the project encountering?
4. Is there anything for me to worry about?
5. Is any action required of me?

Index Cards

This tried-and-true term paper technique allows you to rearrange ideas easily. Simply use one card for each item of information you want to cover, and then sort the cards, arranging them into piles of similar topics.

Sticky Notes or Movable Tape

Like index cards, sticky notes (e.g., Post-its®) and tape allow you to rearrange your ideas easily. Simply write down one idea on each note or strip of tape, and then arrange them on a large piece of paper.

Free Writing

If you can't come up with any ideas using the above methods, try simply writing down whatever comes to mind. For example:

> *Meetings drag on and on. I wonder what we could do to speed them up, make them more efficient. We all talk too much, get off the topic. There goes Steve. Maybe we could get some thoughts from him. An agenda? We don't use one. Time limits? I just talked to Mary, and she said their meetings at the Labor Department have improved. Must check with her to see what they did.*

As you can see, the writer has already generated several ideas about improving meetings. Later, the writer can review the text and use an outline to organize the ideas.

GUIDELINES FOR OUTLINING

Why write an outline?

- The outline provides structure and organization. It illustrates the relationship of ideas.
- It shows you visibly whether you have enough information. For example, if your outline includes only one subheading for a topic, you know that you need to get more data or delete the topic.

- It speeds up the review process when someone in the organization must approve the document. It's much easier to make changes at the outline stage, before you invest time in the draft. And reviewers who approve an outline are much less likely to request major changes later.

Outlines can take several different forms. They can vary from the very informal checklist to the formal Harvard outline.

The Checklist

Use this system to generate and arrange your ideas. The checklist would include a list of words and phrases that cover key points, with space to insert examples, facts, and other supporting material as you go along.

The Semiformal Outline

This is a compromise between the standard outline and the checklist. In this outline, you can show major ideas and the levels of ideas subordinate to them. You may choose to use capitalization, dashes, numbers, indentations, or other means to show the relationships between ideas.

The Traditional Outline

This is the standard (or Harvard) outline. It has a formal framework of Roman and Arabic numerals and uppercase and lowercase letters, arranged with indentations and headings of equal importance. An example might be:

Proposal to make meetings more efficient

- I. Description of the problem
- II. Suggestions for improving meetings
    - A. Agenda
        - 1. Who would be responsible
        - 2. How and when it would be distributed
            - a. Email
            - b. One week before the meeting
    - B. Time limits

The traditional outline can be written by hand or on the computer, using the outline view in Microsoft® Word. The advantage of using a computer in the outlining stage is that it allows you to see your ideas as they occur and to reorganize them easily.

The Electronic Outline

The larger the amount of information you're including in your document, the harder it is to organize. Outlining software can be a useful tool. You can find outlining modules in word processing programs like Microsoft® Word and Corel WordPerfect®, and in presentation packages like Microsoft® PowerPoint. Outlining software packages, including Maxthink and EzOutliner for PCs and OmniOutliner for the Apple® Mac, are also available.

With electronic outlining, you can single out and display all items at the top level of your hierarchy and ignore everything else in your document. This helps you see if your sequence of major topics makes sense. You can also hide or reveal subheads under any major heading. In addition, the software automatically formats for you: You don't have to worry about numbers and letters.

Turning Generated Ideas into an Outline

What are the steps in going from brainstorming techniques like mind mapping, Post-its®, or free writing to writing an outline?

1. Record random ideas quickly into a nonlinear (messy) outline. Use free association to scribble down points.

2. Show relationships. Survey your page of ideas, locate the three or four main points that indicate the direction your document will take, and circle them. Then draw lines to connect these main points to their supporting points.

3. Arrange the points in an order that makes sense.

4. Draft a final outline. Whether you use a Harvard outline (traditional format with Roman numerals, etc.) or a more informal style, you should include the following features:

    - *Depth.* Be sure the entire outline has enough support to develop the draft.

    - *Balance.* Include enough detail for all of your main points. Make sure that each part has at least two subdivisions.

    - *Parallel form.* Give points in the same grouping the same grammatical form. For example, use either topics or complete sentences for all of your points.

Writing an Outline after the Draft

If you have a difficult time developing an outline, an alternative plan is to write your outline after writing your first draft. Read through your draft and jot down in the margin, next to each paragraph, the main thought in that paragraph. If you find that the paragraph doesn't seem to have a main thought, or has too many of them, make a note of that. Then read back over those margin notes, and figure out which paragraphs fit together in big sections and which are smaller subsections. Write an outline of what you see. Writing such an outline lets you examine the skeleton of your document and figure out what the outline of the next draft should be.

Whatever system you use to generate and organize your ideas, don't hesitate to revise and reorganize the outline as the writing proceeds. An outline is only a guide, and you should not feel constricted by it.

GUIDELINES FOR SEQUENCING YOUR IDEAS

After you've generated ideas and produced some kind of an outline, check over your outline to make sure that you've put your ideas in the best order for impact. When you use the appropriate method of development, your readers are drawn to your ideas and can follow your line of thought. Below are the most common ways to sequence your ideas, depending on whether the goal is to inform or to persuade.

Documents to Inform

- *Inverted pyramid.* Memo announcing a meeting. Give the most important information first.

- *Order of familiarity.* Explanation of how a new system or product operates. Go from the most familiar to the least.

- *Order of location.* Description of new office building. Use spatial or geographic order.
- *Alphabetical order.* Biographies of new employees.
- *Chronological order.* Annual reports, minutes of meetings, case histories.
- *Category order.* Deals with topics that go together. Classifies ideas into reasonable categories.
- *Inductive order.* Articles for trade publications. Go from specific examples to generalized conclusions.
- *List.* Memo to boss giving projects you're working on.
- *Order for comparison.* Two or more ideas, products, places, or employees. You have two choices: (1) point-by-point comparison or (2) block comparison.
- *Deductive order.* Memo explaining a new idea, such as why you need new computer software. Start with the general principle and support it with examples.

Documents to Persuade

- *Statement of reasons method.* This method is very similar to the category order method for documents to inform, except that each main point is a reason why your readers should accept and agree with your point of view.

- *Comparative advantages method.* As you look at a list of reasons why your readers should accept your point of view, you might see that the best reasons are phrased as advantages over the procedure now in practice.

- *Problem-solution method.* The main points should be formulated to show that:

  - There is a problem that requires a change in attitude or behavior.

  - The solution you are presenting will solve the problem.

  - Your solution is the best possible solution to this particular problem.

- *Most acceptable to least acceptable.* This order is useful when you know or can predict what the reader is likely to accept or reject.

TEST YOURSELF

SELECTING THE PURPOSE AND SEQUENCE

Read the following paragraphs. Select the paragraph that states the purpose. Put a "1" next to it. Then use the numbers 2, 3, 4, and 5 to indicate the appropriate sequence for the remaining paragraphs of the letter.

We will occupy the entire eighth and ninth floors. To reach the reception area, take the lobby elevator and go to the eighth floor. When you get there, someone will show you to your office. Most of the sales offices will be on that floor, while other offices, including research and development, as well as finance and administration, will be on the ninth floor.

The address of the building is 700 Market Street, which is between Maple Avenue and Grant Street. The building is a large, 10-story brick building set back from the street.

Most of the offices will have the new desks, chairs, and bookcases that you selected. Some offices will include additional chairs and tables.

We are happy to announce that our new headquarters are ready for occupancy. We have scheduled the move for September 25. Before then, however, we would like each of you to visit the new offices.

Please check your office and make sure everything you ordered is there. We look forward to hearing from you and hope you will let us know of anything you need.

What ordering system would you use to organize these paragraphs? See the Appendix for the answer and a suggested revision of the letter.

Writing can proceed much more easily if you understand the phases in the writing process: (1) planning, (2) drafting, and (3) editing. Each phase should be distinct and separate. During the *planning* stage, you must understand the purpose, the audience or reader, and the subject of the document. To make sure you understand the purpose, get as much guidance as possible at the beginning of your project.

Readers can be categorized according to their roles: managers, experts or advisors, operators, and general readers or laypersons. For each of these reader categories, you need to determine the decision-making level, knowledge of the subject, type or form of information needed, and likely reaction to what you write. If you are writing for a diverse audience, you need to speak to both primary and secondary readers. To understand your subject, make sure you collect and analyze relevant information.

Once you've determined your purpose, audience, and subject, you're ready to produce an outline. You may start with a nonlinear form, then determine relationships and the order of the topics. Once you do that, you're ready to create a formal or semiformal outline. This is a "working outline," which you might want to change as you draft your document.

NOTES

1 Plain Language Action and Information Network, "Identify and write for your audience." Online at http://www.plainlanguage.gov (accessed March 2007).
2 Plain Language Action and Information Network, "Using Writer-Friendly Documents." Online at http://www.plainlanguage.gov (accessed March 2007).
3 Maryann V. Piotowski, *Effective Business Writing: A Guide for Those Who Write on the Job* (New York: Harper Collins, 1996), 7–8.
4 Tony Buzan, *The Mind Map Book* (New York: Penguin, 1991).

CHAPTER 3

Drafting: Writing It Down

◆ **Getting It Down on Paper** ◆

Tom began to write the first draft of his recommendation of Marcia Thompson. One of his paragraphs read as follows:

> *I have always been impressed by Marcia's thoroughness, adherence to quality, and honesty. Her honesty extends from areas where we easily see it (in relationships and business transactions) to integrity of thought. Scientific, thorough, and meticulous, she approaches any analytical task with an exacting eye. This is what I mean by integrity of thought. She also is helpful and pleasant to work with, in fact, she takes the time to help those who are learning their way.*

"What do you think of this paragraph?" Tom asked his colleague, Brad.

"Well, it has some good points," Brad said. "You explained what you meant by honesty and provided good examples of Marcia's honesty. Also, you used varied sentence structure. Some of your sentences are long and some are short. One of them begins with a phrase ('Scientific, thorough, and meticulous') instead of the standard subject-verb format.

"However, I would change a couple of things. I think you try to cover too many topics in this paragraph. It doesn't seem unified. Perhaps you could discuss only Marcia's honesty in this paragraph and discuss her helpfulness in another. Also, you have a run-on sentence. You need to put a period or semicolon after 'pleasant to work with.'"

"Hey, thanks so much," Tom said. "You've been really helpful."

Chapter 2 focused on how to organize your writing in a general way. Now that you know what you're going to write, the ideas to include, and the order in which to include them, it's time to put your plan into action.

This vignette illustrates two important features of a first draft: paragraphs and sentences. This chapter will discuss how to organize the paragraphs and structure the sentences in your writing.

TURNING OFF YOUR INNER CRITIC

Remember, you are writing your *first draft*. You are not aiming to produce a perfect document on the first try. If you attempt to do so, you may find yourself facing paralysis and frustration because you are trying to do two very different things—write and edit—at once. So turn off the your inner critic and give your creative self the freedom to write without constraint.

Plunge into your first draft with the goal of getting something down on paper or on your computer screen. Leave concerns about tone, word choice, spelling, and grammar to the editing stage. Right now, the most important thing is to get into the flow of writing. If you can't think of a particular word to use, leave a blank space. You can always fill it in later.

GETTING STARTED ON YOUR FIRST DRAFT

Deborah Dumaine, in her book *Write to the Top: Writing for Corporate Success*, recommends three steps to take in moving from your outline to your first draft:[1]

1. Take each topic in your outline and create a headline for it. Begin with the topic that you feel most comfortable with. You don't need to write your first draft in order.

2. Take each headline and write a paragraph for it. The headline becomes the topic sentence of the paragraph.

3. Add new headings as you need them, and then write the paragraphs to go with them.

Use whatever writing technique is easiest for you. For example, you might try one of the following:[2]

- Set a timer and start writing. Write as quickly as you can, sticking to the ideas in your outline.
- Go to the outline (list of headings) in your computer. Write a paragraph for each headline in any order. Then print out what you have drafted to see how it looks on paper.
- If speaking is easier than writing for you, try dictating your first draft. Then transcribe what you have dictated to see how it looks.

PLANNING PARAGRAPHS

Paragraphs are groups of related sentences set off as distinct sections. They serve several purposes. A well-written paragraph helps the reader by breaking down complex ideas into manageable parts, focusing attention on one idea at a time, and relating each part to the main idea of the document. Paragraphs focus attention on important points. They also give variety to your page by breaking up long blocks of text.

A well-developed paragraph does not need to be long. *Paragraphs should be long enough to make their point adequately—and no longer.* The trend today is toward shorter paragraphs, just as it is toward shorter sentences. Use your eye to monitor paragraph length. If a paragraph turns a page into a mass of gray, find a way to break it into shorter paragraphs. If your paragraph is more than 10 to 12 lines (about 2 inches), consider breaking it into two or more paragraphs, even if it develops a single idea. Many writers recommend that paragraphs be no longer than five or six lines.

Using the headline-writing technique will help you get started on writing paragraphs.

QUALITIES OF EFFECTIVE PARAGRAPHS

Effective paragraphs have several characteristics:

- *Unity.* Each element of the paragraph contributes to the main idea; nothing irrelevant appears.

- *Coherence.* The parts of the paragraph relate clearly to each other, with each element leading logically to the next.

- *Development.* The main idea is well supported with details—facts, examples, and reasons.

Unity

The PLAIN website says this about paragraphing:

> *Limiting each paragraph to one issue gives the document a clean appearance and contributes to the impression that it is easy to read and understand. By presenting only one issue in each paragraph, you can use informative headings that reflect the entire issue covered by the paragraph.*[3]

Limiting each paragraph to one topic also is a way of making sure that the reader doesn't miss or confuse your main points. Tacking on a second idea at the end of a paragraph, or burying one in the middle, can have three negative consequences:

- The reader might fail to grasp the importance of the second idea.
- The reader might be distracted from the first idea, which is the actual topic of the paragraph.
- The reader might get the impression that your thinking is muddled.

The Need for a Topic Sentence

The *topic sentence* summarizes and introduces what a paragraph is all about. You can think of a paragraph as a symphony movement; the topic sentence is the major theme, and the rest of the paragraph is the development of that theme.

Your reader is usually best served if you put the topic sentence first in the paragraph. This practice shortens reading time. The reader does not have to look through the paragraph to find its main point. Also, the reader can skim the topic sentences of all the paragraphs to get the gist of the entire document. Again, think of the inverted pyramid: Put the most important information on top.

Consider the following example:

> *We have two criteria for the equipment: economy and size. It is necessary that the equipment be economical; we cannot invest more than $200. It is also important that it fit into the space we have available—2 feet by 3 feet by 3 feet.*

Here the main criteria for the equipment are stated in a topic sentence at the outset of the paragraph. Then the body of the paragraph explains why these criteria are being used and specifies them in dollars and space.

In some cases, it might not be best to put the topic sentence first. For example, you might want to begin your paragraph with a transition sentence that ties the paragraph to the preceding one. In these cases, the topic sentence should be the second sentence.

Also, putting the topic sentence later in the paragraph is sometimes better when you have to convey bad news. This indirect approach prepares the reader for the unpleasantness. In most situations, however, it is best to say what you have to say first and explain it later.

How to Develop the Topic Sentence

If you have already written a paragraph and need to create a topic sentence for it, you might take the approach suggested by Judson Monroe in *Effective Research and Report Writing in Government*:[4]

1. Identify the main idea of your paragraph. Ask yourself, "What am I trying to say in this paragraph?"

2. Write down a headline sentence—the simplest form of your main idea that you can think of.

3. Write the entire sentence by answering the following questions:

    - Who?

    - What?

    - When?

    - Where?

- Why?
- How?

4. Refer to the headline whenever you need to. For example:

   - *Headline:* Taxes are due.
   - *Question:* What kind of taxes?
   - *Sentence:* Corporation taxes are due.
   - *Question:* When?
   - *Sentence:* Corporation taxes are due within 60 days of fiscal closing.
   - *Question:* Why? (or, under what conditions?)
   - *Sentence:* Because of a new regulation governing the timing of tax payments, corporation taxes are now due within 60 days of fiscal closing.
   - *Question:* Where?
   - *Sentence:* Corporation taxes are due to the Virginia Department of Taxation within 60 days of fiscal closing.
   - *Question:* How?

- *Sentence*: Corporation taxes can be filed online, by telephone using a credit card, or through the regular post.

In developing the paragraph, you might need to do the work in two stages:

1. Put down your thoughts in the order that they come to you.

2. Change that order.

Here is a paragraph that reflects the flow of its writer's initial thinking process:

> *The ADSI 1000 Electronic Printing System consists of an input subsystem, either a tape transport for offline printing or an interface unit for online operations, a control subsystem for processing and displaying and storing digital data, a subsystem that produces the image, and an output subsystem that routes sheets to an output stacker bin at the rate of three sheets per second. This rate is 50 percent faster than that of the ADSI's nearest competitor. In fact, the ADSI is the fastest system of its kind on the market.*

The writer's main point—the selling point—appears all the way at the bottom of the paragraph instead of at the top. The writer has worked up to it. To be effective, the paragraph needs to be turned around so that it starts off with this main point:

The ADSI is the fastest system of its kind on the market—50 percent faster than its nearest competitor.

The following are examples of effective topic sentences:

- Ginnie Maes can provide worry-free investment income.
- Capital spending increased dramatically in November.
- The new software program provides three major benefits.

Coherence

A paragraph is coherent if the reader can see how it holds together without having to puzzle out the writer's reasons for adding each new sentence. Within a paragraph, as within an entire written message, there should be a logical movement or progression.

Expressing Elements of a Paragraph Consistently

Your paragraph will be more coherent if you maintain the same person and tense throughout the paragraph.

- *Person.* Switching from "you" to "one" to "he" can be very disconcerting to the reader, as the following example illustrates:

For example, if you are a law student, you may already know that you want a job with a corporate law firm. Those who are business students may know that their aim is to enter executive training programs as the first step in retailing careers. If the person is getting an advanced degree in art history, however, he or she may be somewhat less clear about their goal.

- *Tense.* Maintain the same tense for the same subject within a paragraph; for example, events in the past should not be described in the present tense and also in the past tense. Use the present tense whenever you can. If the events you are discussing have taken place over a period of time, use a sequence of tenses to make the time relationships clear.

  Confusing:

  If your time log has shown that most of your interruptions were from people around you, obviously you are not going to be able to solve the problem by controlling incoming calls.

  Better:

  If your time log shows that most of your interruptions are from people around you, obviously you can't solve the problem by controlling incoming calls.

Using Transitional Devices for Continuity

Conjunctions (such as "and," "but," and "or") and *transition words* (such as "therefore" and "however") help readers follow the flow of ideas in a paragraph or between paragraphs. The following are some relationships and the transition words that can express them:

- *Contrast*—however, although, but, conversely, nevertheless, yet, still, on the other hand, even so, even though, in contrast, in spite of, on the contrary, regardless, otherwise
- *Comparison*—similarly, likewise, in the same way
- *Cause and effect*—as a result, therefore, consequently, thus, so, because
- *Example*—for instance, for example, specifically, as an illustration
- *Addition*—moreover, besides, in addition, also, too, furthermore
- *Time*—now, later, after, before, meanwhile, following, then
- *Sequence*—first, second, third, next, last, finally
- *Place*—further on, above, below, nearly, on the left, behind, around
- *Repetition or summation*—all in all, in conclusion, in summary, in other words

Using Reference Words and Repetition for Linkage

Use reference words such as "this," "that," "these," "those," and other demonstrative pronouns to tie in new ideas with points made earlier. Also, link your ideas by repeating the topic or key words. For example, if you are writing a report on the benefits of a software program, you might repeat the word "benefit" in each paragraph as a cue to the reader that you are continuing the main idea.

Development

A paragraph can be unified and coherent but still be inadequate. This is because some writers fail to substantiate ideas with supporting facts and explanations. Their readers become interested in the subject, only to be disappointed when no further information is provided. Other writers get so carried away with a subject that they give too much information and bore their readers.

You need to find a way to develop your ideas adequately but not excessively.

A well-developed paragraph provides the specific information that readers need and expect to understand you and to stay interested in what you're saying. You might want to develop and arrange the information according to a specific pattern.

The patterns of paragraph development are similar to those for overall development of your document. The following are some of these patterns:

- *Chronological or sequential* (first, next, last). Especially useful when explaining procedures, spelling out an action plan, or narrating a sequence of events.
- *Geographical* (north to south, basement to top floor, etc.). Useful when describing or analyzing an organization's activity, area by area.
- *Size* (largest to smallest, or smallest to largest). Useful in explaining some procedures or in selling some ideas for change.
- *Familiar to unfamiliar.* Helpful when explaining new ideas or procedures, or when selling an idea that might threaten the reader (if only because it is new and different).
- *Most acceptable to least acceptable.* Useful when you know or can predict what the reader is likely to accept or reject.
- *General to specific.* Useful when you want to (1) state a principle and then give examples or (2) state a rule and then give exceptions. You make the general statement and follow it with specific examples, limitations, qualifications, exclusions, or modifications.

TEST YOURSELF

ORGANIZING PARAGRAPHS

A. Putting the Main Idea Up Front and Cutting Ideas that Don't Belong

Read over the seven sentences that follow. Then decide how you would make a unified, well-planned paragraph out of them.

Two of the sentences do not contribute to the topic being discussed. Cross them out.

The remaining five sentences can be rearranged to form a coherent paragraph. Decide how you would arrange them to put the main idea up front and give the paragraph a logical order of development. Number the sentences 1 to 5, with the topic sentence number 1, the next sentence number 2, and so on.

____ As we took the bag from the shipping container, the bag broke open.

____ The only problem was minor, and it occurred when we removed one of the samples from its shipping container.

____ Three of the scientists were unable to make it to our planning meeting and were not aware of our timeline.

____ The entire lab procedure went as planned.

____ Fortunately, we had an extra sample from that same location.

____ The sample shattered when it fell onto the table.

____ During our last lab procedure, we did not have extra samples.

B. Making New Paragraphs

Expressed in a single paragraph, the material that follows looks massive and uninviting. How would you break it up into five paragraphs? Indicate where you would make paragraph breaks by inserting paragraph symbols (¶).

The term "white paper" originated in the early 20th century in England. This type of writing was used to differentiate short government position papers from longer, more detailed reports. The shorter position papers were bound in white covers, while the longer reports were bound in blue covers. Now white papers are rarely bound and have evolved into more versatile documents. So what exactly is a white paper in today's business world? Although there is no exhaustive definition covering the wide range of papers called white papers, the most comprehensive definition is "a communication tool used to explain something complex to an audience with little to no background on the topic." Research shows that people use white papers as means of first learning about a given topic or product. A common thread among white papers is the use of a problem and solution. Rather than beginning by just naming the merits of a product or service like a marketing brochure, the white paper usually highlights a problem that is common with the target audience. After clearly outlining a problem, a good white paper shows how the reader can use the product or service to solve the problem. White papers work well as a marketing tool for many reasons. Besides being very industry-specific and consumer-focused, white papers make great justifications for customers wanting to purchase the service or product. There is no better way for employees to explain the need for a product or service to their bosses than presenting a well-written document by an industry expert clearly outlining the problems and the benefits. It grabs attention initially and has a strong pull all the way to the point of sale. The single industry where white papers proliferate is information technology. The industry changes so fast that IT professionals constantly face new problems and solutions. White papers play a vital role in this industry by helping both marketers and customers. Most IT websites have hundreds of white papers available for download, and the best part is that they are almost always free.

See the Appendix for answers.

TEST YOURSELF

WRITING TOPIC SENTENCES

Add a topic sentence to the beginning of each of the following paragraphs:

1. *The first characteristic is the audience's decision-making level or degree of influence. A second characteristic of audiences is their knowledge of the subject. Finally, the writer should consider the type or form of information that the audience needs.*
2. *We selected Barbara because of her experience as a team leader. John seemed a good choice for the ABC Project because of his technical skills. Finally, we chose Cheryl because of her years of experience and her knowledge of the procedures.*

See the Appendix for answers.

WRITING SENTENCES

Whenever you express a complete thought or feeling, and name something and tell something about it, you are writing a *sentence*.

In its simplest form, a sentence has two essential elements: a subject and a predicate.

The subject is who or what the sentence is about. Sometimes the subject of a sentence is *implied* rather than actually *stated*. In giving instructions, for example, you might say, "Turn left at the end of the hall." What you are really saying is, "You turn left at the end of the hall." The "you" is implied. Note that many of the sentences in this handbook, including this one, are written in this way.

The predicate is the part of the sentence that says something about the subject. For example, in the sentence, "The Computer Support Department looks forward to providing network assistance to the agency," the predicate is "looks forward to providing network assistance to the agency."

Sentence Fragments

Sentences must be complete. A *sentence fragment* is a part of a sentence that is set off as if it were a whole sentence. Unlike a complete sentence, a sentence fragment lacks a subject, a predicate, or both, or it is a subordinate clause not attached to a complete sentence.

Fragment: *The new employees and their mentors. (lacks a predicate)*

Fragment: *Will meet tomorrow. (lacks a subject)*

Sentence: *The new employees and their mentors will meet tomorrow.*

Fragment: *After the new employees and their mentors meet tomorrow. (is a subordinate clause)*

Sentence: *After the new employees and their mentors meet tomorrow, we will have a better idea of how to structure our training program.*

Run-On Sentences

Careless writers often fall into another kind of error with sentences. They write *run-on sentences,* in which two main clauses are joined by only a comma with no connecting word.

> *"Meet me at the office at nine, I'll be waiting for you."*
>
> *"There are those who will tell you my job is easy, don't believe them, they have no idea what I do."*

The sentences above are incorrect. The following are corrected versions of each:

> *"Meet me at the office at nine. I'll be waiting for you."*
>
> *"There are those who will tell you my job is easy. Don't believe them because they have no idea what I do."*

Conjunctive Adverbs

One group of words—conjunctive adverbs—often causes problems in sentence structure. The following are conjunctive adverbs, words that describe the relation of ideas in two clauses.

- accordingly
- also
- anyway
- besides
- certainly
- consequently
- finally
- further
- furthermore
- hence
- however
- incidentally
- indeed
- instead
- likewise
- meanwhile
- moreover
- namely
- nevertheless
- next
- nonetheless
- now
- otherwise
- similarly
- still
- then
- thereafter
- therefore
- thus
- undoubtedly

Unlike coordinating conjunctions such as "and," "but," "or," "nor," "so," "yet," and "for," conjunctive adverbs don't bind two clauses into a grammatical unit. Note the following:

- The document was quite long; *consequently*, I spent a long time reading it.
- The document was quite long, *and* I spent a long time reading it.

Place a **semicolon, not a comma**, before the conjunctive adverb.

There is a simple test to distinguish a conjunctive adverb from a coordinating conjunction. Because a conjunctive adverb is an adverb, it can be moved elsewhere in the sentence.

- The document was quite long; I *consequently* spent a long time reading it.

But you can't move the coordinating conjunction.

- The document was quite long, *and* I spent a long time reading it.

Overloaded Sentences

The following sentence is not, strictly speaking, grammatically incorrect. But it does impede the reader's understanding by piling up too many ideas, one after the other.

> *The statements were made by Richard N. Wilson, Project Director for the Southern Regional Center, a federally funded, department-sponsored project that does research for participating agencies in Region IV, a region that includes Kentucky, Tennessee, North Carolina, South Carolina, Georgia, Alabama, Mississippi, and Florida.*

The writer of this sentence has ignored natural stopping places and has tied together ideas that should be expressed in separate sentences. Shorter sentences break the information into smaller, easier-to-process units. Therefore, they are better for conveying complex information. Vary your sentences to avoid choppiness, but don't revert to overloaded sentences like this.

TEST YOURSELF

OVERLOADED SENTENCES

Rewrite the following sentence to make it clearer:

The National Transportation Safety Board today announced that it has completed an investigation of the midair collision of a commercial plane and a twin-engine private plane, which resulted in the deaths of 34 people, and the investigation showed that, immediately before impact, the private plane had made a 360-degree roll, and that both planes had been in an air corridor that was restricted to oncoming commercial flights, and the board concluded that, in all probability, the accident was the result of pilot error.

See the Appendix for answers.

Choppy Sentences

Choppiness results from too many short sentences, lack of sentence transition, and unvaried sentence patterns. Such writing can be monotonous and even irritating because we all need variety.

> *Read this paragraph out loud. It sounds choppy. The style seems immature. It sounds as if it was written by an 8-year-old. The writing is boring. It is monotonous.*[5]

Contrast the paragraph above with the following paragraph:

> *If you read this paragraph out loud, you'll realize that it sounds choppy. The style seems immature, as though it were written by an 8-year-old. It's boring and monotonous.*[6]

To overcome choppiness, try the following:

- Vary sentence beginnings. The first paragraph above sounds choppy because most of the sentences begin with the subject. To alleviate this repetitious pattern, try one of the following suggestions:

  - Open with a descriptive word (a modifier). "Strangely, the government did not give liberal leave during last week's snow storm."

  - Open with a descriptive phrase (a modifier). "Despite my better judgment, I let Harold take over the project."

  - Open with a subordinate clause (a dependent word group with a subject and verb). "When Congress announced its budget reform package, members of both political parties offered their support."

  - Open with an infinitive ("to" plus a verb). "To protect our resources, we must make recycling a way of life."

- Vary the placement of transitions (words and phrases that link ideas).

  - Place the transition at the beginning: "In addition, providing child care in the workplace is a good idea because half of all mothers work."

– Place it in the middle: "Jan's opinion, on the other hand, is that child-care programs will cost too much money."

– Place it at the end: "Many employers now offer day care as a benefit, however."

- Combine short sentences that relate in content.

  – *(Before)* "The Recreation Division will close its Central City offices next fall. The closing will occur because of downsizing."

  – *(After)* "Next fall, because of downsizing, the Recreation Division will close its Central City offices."

- Vary the length of your sentences.

  – "This office needs a director who knows how to deal effectively with upper management and how to trim waste from the budget. This office needs Lee Johnson."

  – Use your ear. Read your paragraphs aloud. When you hear that the sentences are not flowing well, place a check mark. Then go back and use the techniques just described to ease the flow.[7]

TEST YOURSELF

SOUND SENTENCES

A. Classifying Sentences

Some of the following sentences are complete. Others are run-on sentences, while others are sentence fragments. In front of the number for each sentence, put the symbol that applies:

C for complete sentence

R for run-on sentence

F for sentence fragment

1. Although we found that the committee had many constructive and appealing ideas.
2. John plans to graduate from college next year, furthermore, he wants to go to graduate school the following year.
3. Don't forget to see the exhibit at the art gallery; it will be closing in another two weeks.
4. Never in my life had I been so frightened.
5. The students, studying furiously, trying to cram in as much information as possible before the exam.
6. The Redskins beat the Cowboys?
7. If you do not give us your answer by the end of the week, we will have to assume you are not interested in the position.
8. The Gladys Porter Zoo, located in Brownsville, which is located in the southern tip of Texas.
9. Go.
10. Hoping all is well with you.

B. Complete the Sentence

Make complete sentences out of these fragments:

11. Sir Alexander Fleming, an immunologist, whose reputation as the discoverer of penicillin almost rivals that of Jonas Salk, who invented the polio vaccine.
12. Sue cooked dinner. While Rudy cleaned the house.
13. Although the case had been closed for 17 years. The investigators found new evidence.
14. Sam is a good friend. Whose advice I have valued over the years.
15. The auto mechanic assured us the repairs would be minor. Then proceeded to list a dozen things wrong with the car.
16. The employees quit their jobs. Finding that they could no longer work under such stressful conditions and with so few benefits.
17. Police chiefs want to hire more officers. However, not without additional funds.

C. Using Punctuation in Sentences

Insert or substitute proper punctuation to remedy these run-on sentences:

18. On the one hand, he is a careful worker, on the other hand, he takes too long to complete his assignments.
19. You can count on Mark to help you out, he's very reliable.
20. There are two reasons why you should take that trip to Atlanta, one is to meet with the regional director and the other is to check on our suppliers.

See the Appendix for answers.

TEST YOURSELF

REWRITING TOM'S LETTER

Reread the vignette at the beginning of this chapter. Take the suggestions given by Brad and rewrite Tom's paragraph. A suggested paragraph is given in the Appendix.

TIPS FOR WRITING DRAFTS

In his book, *A Pocket Guide to Technical Writing*, William S. Pfeiffer recommends the following:[8]

- Once you have a complete outline in hand, write your first draft quickly.
- Schedule blocks of drafting time. Do whatever is needed to prevent being interrupted for at least 30 to 60 minutes.
- Don't stop to edit.
- Begin with the easiest section.
- Write summaries last.

How to Avoid Writer's Block

You might find that you become stuck while writing your first draft. You might reach a point where you can't seem to go on. To avoid wasting time during this stage of the writing process, try these tips:

- Change your environment—find a quiet place with no distractions.
- Take a break and come back to your task refreshed.
- Start writing the section of the document that comes most easily or, depending on your makeup, the section that is most difficult. In either case, do not feel you must write down your ideas in the order in which they will ultimately appear.
- If possible, avoid writing when you are emotionally or mentally preoccupied or physically fatigued.
- Find the time of day and the place that you do your best writing.
- Promise yourself a reward for your hard work.

Getting Some Distance from Your Draft

After you finish writing your first draft, walk away from it. It's difficult to be objective when you're too close to your writing. In a perfect world, you would have the time to put your draft aside and revisit it in a day or two—but this is not a perfect world, and we seldom have the time to do this. However, even a ten- to 15-minute break can make a difference. When you're pressed for time, try one of the following:

- Try to clear your mind for a few moments. Visualize the site of your last vacation.
- Go for a short walk—even if it's just down the hall and back.
- Get a cup of coffee or a soft drink.
- Make a quick telephone call about a completely different project.

Revisiting the Draft

After you get some distance, it's time to be more critical. Then you can look at the overall draft and check a few things *before* going into the editing stage. Take a minute to assess the following:

- Did I explain my purpose clearly?
- Did I consider the role, knowledge level, attitude, and other characteristics of the reader?
- Does the overall organization of the draft make sense?
- Did I provide closure? (For example, did you tell readers exactly what you want them to do?)

During the drafting stage, it's important to work quickly and freely and to let your ideas flow. This means resisting any temptation to edit as you write.

Focus on paragraphing—making sure that your paragraphs are unified, coherent, and well developed. You also want to look at your sentences to make sure they are correct, concise, and smooth.

During the drafting stage, you might find yourself at an impasse. Writers frequently experience this feeling of writer's block, and they deal with it in a variety of ways.

After you have completed your draft, get some distance before looking at it critically. After taking a cursory look at your first draft, you're ready to go on to the editing stage.

NOTES

1 Deborah Dumaine, *Write to the Top: Writing for Corporate Success* (New York: Random House, 1989), 77–78.
2 Ibid., 60–62.
3 Plain Language Action and Information Network, "Include Only One Issue in Each Paragraph." Online at http://www.plainlanguage.gov (accessed January 2008).
4 Judson Monroe, *Effective Research and Report Writing in Government* (New York: McGraw-Hill, 1980).
5 Barbara Fine Clouse, *Working It Out: A Troubleshooting Guide for Writers*, 2nd ed. (New York: McGraw-Hill, 1997), 90.
6 Ibid.
7 Ibid., 91–93.
8 William S. Pfeiffer, *A Pocket Guide to Technical Writing* (New York: IDG Books, 2003), 12–13.

CHAPTER 4

Editing: Using the Right Voice and Tone

◆ Setting the Tone ◆

"I'm working on a section of our office handbook, and I have a draft for you to read," said Greg, Maria's coworker. "It just doesn't sound right. Perhaps you can offer some suggestions."

Maria had recently spent time reviewing books on business writing and was feeling more confident about her writing skills. She sat down and read the following document:

> *It has been noted that employees in this agency are spending excessive amounts of time on the Internet during regular working hours. This practice has been observed to have increased in the past year. All employees need to stop this practice immediately or severe measures will be taken. If any part of this message is not clear, please call the Director's office and it will be explained.*

"You can improve this in two ways," Maria told Greg. "First, try to use a friendlier tone. Then, change the passive voice to the active voice."

Greg came back a little later and showed Maria the following revision:

> *We'd like to ask your cooperation in helping to make our agency more productive. Please limit your use of the Internet to searches that are directly related to your job. In addition, please try to make Internet searches efficient. Schedule specific amounts of time for yourself—preferably no more than a half-hour at a time.*
>
> *Although the Internet is a valuable tool for research and communication, it can also be a distraction. If you have any questions about Internet use, please call the Director's office.*

"That's a great improvement," said Maria, who was happy with the success of her first writing assignment. "Now maybe they won't feel like throwing things at us."

Now that you have words on paper, it's time to edit your work. You might not be able to send your writing to the copy desk, but you can turn a critical eye on yourself. The best plan is to put your first draft away for a while before you begin to edit it. This allows you to look at it from a fresh perspective. Or, ask someone whose writing you admire to look it over.

As you can see from the scenario just described, voice and tone can either strengthen or weaken the impact of writing. Using the active voice, selecting strong verbs, and deciding on the right tone can make a world of difference in your business writing. In this chapter, you'll learn how to recognize and correct problems in these areas.

WRITING TIP: PREFER THE ACTIVE VOICE

We often lessen the impact of our writing by using the passive voice.

In an active sentence, the person or agency performing an action is the subject of the sentence. In a passive sentence, the person or item acted upon is the subject of the sentence.

Changing passive voice to active voice in your writing can add energy and cut wordiness. William Zinsser has this advice: "Use active verbs unless there is no comfortable way to get around using a passive verb. The difference between an active-verb style and a passive-verb style—in clarity and vigor—is the difference between life and death for a writer."[1]

Consider the following two versions of the same basic message, which describes a supervisor:

> *All issues and questions were discussed and explained very clearly by my supervisor. Following the comple-*

tion of each task, I received a full feedback that gave me an opportunity to reflect upon and improve my performance. I was given support in addressing my personal objectives such as improvement of interviewing skills and building technical and client knowledge.

My supervisor clearly explained all the issues and fully answered my questions. His comments after every task helped me to reflect upon and improve my performance. He constantly encouraged me to address my objectives, such as improving my interviewing skills and building my technical knowledge.

The first version, in passive voice, is wordier, weaker, and less direct. The second version, in active voice, is briefer, clearer, and more conversational or natural.

How to Recognize Passive and Active Sentences

The active voice emphasizes who is doing something:

- *"My supervisor clearly explained all the issues and fully answered my questions."*

The actor (my supervisor) comes first in the sentence. That subject of the sentence does the action.

The passive voice shows who or what is being acted upon:

- *"All issues and questions were discussed and explained very clearly by my supervisor."*

Passive sentences have two basic features, though they do not occur in every passive sentence:

- Some form of the verb "to be" as a helping verb
- A past participle (usually with "ed" on the end)

Passive voice:

- "The checks *have been* mailed."
- "Regulations *have been proposed* by the Department of Veterans Affairs."
- "You *were asked* by me."
- "Copies *are prepared* downstairs."

Active voice:

- "We *mailed* the checks."
- "We *have proposed* regulations."
- "I *asked* you."
- "Mark and Heather *prepare* copies downstairs."

Often the word "by" appears after the verb to show who performs the action of the verb.

- Passive voice: "The speech was given by the director."
- Active voice: "The director gave the speech."

The Case for the Active Voice

For the following reasons, you should use the active voice for most sentences:

1. A sentence with an active verb form sounds more natural; the active voice is the way we usually think and speak.

    - *Passive*: "The meal was enjoyed by us."

    - *Active*: "We enjoyed the meal."

2. The active voice is more vigorous and direct. The passive voice makes writing weak.

- *Passive*: "An excellent job was done by Stacy."

- *Active*: "Stacy did an excellent job."

- *Passive*: "Many complaints are heard about the working conditions."

- *Active*: "Many people complain about the working conditions."

3. The passive voice can be confusing, especially in sentences like this one:

- *Passive*: "A Department of Health survey of the screening clinic at University Hospital was made."

  The sentence above doesn't tell us who conducted the survey. In the active voice, all doubts are removed:

- *Active*: "The Department of Health surveyed the screening clinic at University Hospital."

4. The passive voice adds length to writing. Look back over the samples. In each case, the sentence in the active voice is shorter than the sentence in the passive voice.

5. Sentences with active verbs make the writer seem confident; sentences with passive verbs sound evasive, show an unwillingness to accept or assign responsibility, and often give less information.

   - *Passive*: "The decision was made to eliminate employee bonuses."

   - *Active*: "The director decided to eliminate employee bonuses."

The Case for the Passive Voice

The passive voice can be used occasionally:

1. When one action follows another as a matter of law, and there is no actor (besides the law itself) for the second action

   - *Passive:* "If you do not pay the royalty on your mineral production, your lease will be terminated [by the action of the law]."[2]

2. To move the important element to the front of the sentence where it will have greater prominence than in the middle or at the end

    - *Passive*: "A fixed-price contract bid must be submitted to the office by May 5."

    - *Passive*: "The President was released from the hospital."

3. To point out an error or shortcoming in a diplomatic way

    - *Passive*: "An error was made in the last set of calculations."

    - *Passive*: "It seems that the situation could have been better handled by the review staff."

4. In cases when the agents performing the action are unknown, unidentifiable, or unimportant

    - *Passive*: "The three-dimensional model is cut out of nylon."

    - *Passive*: "It has been shown that people tend to look away while they are speaking."

How to Activate Passive Sentences

To communicate effectively, write most of your sentences in the active voice. To change passive sentences to active, follow these four steps:

1. Find or supply the actor(s).
    - "An excellent job was done by Stacy." *Stacy* is the actor.
2. Put the actor at the beginning of the sentence.
    - "Stacy . . ."
3. Replace the passive verb with an active verb.
    - "Stacy did . . ."
4. Make the subject of the passive sentence the direct object.
    - "Stacy did an excellent job."

TEST YOURSELF

CHANGING PASSIVE VOICE TO ACTIVE VOICE

Rewrite the following sentences. Change passive voice to active voice. Say things as directly as you can. Supply the subject of the sentence when necessary.

1. Leslie Brooks was chosen Employee of the Year by the managers.
2. We were given an escorted tour of the jail by the police.
3. Was that film recommended by the reviewers?
4. A presentation was given to our agency by the software company.
5. An explanation of how to sell a product was given by the guest speaker.
6. An incorrect version of the policy had been distributed by the accounting department.
7. It became clear that the facts were misrepresented by the witnesses.
8. It is recommended by the police that you stick to the main roads.
9. Has he been rehired?
10. Your help is appreciated.
11. A college degree and five years of experience are required for the job.
12. It has been determined by the investigating committee that the nomination should be withdrawn.

See the Appendix for answers.

WRITING TIP: BRING SUBMERGED ACTION TO THE SURFACE

Verbs give action to sentences. *Submerged verbs* are those combined with auxiliary or other weak verbs and turned into nouns. Submerged verbs often occur in connection with the weak verbs "to be," "to make," and "to do."

- Weak: "The accountants do careful work in getting out the final numbers."
- Stronger: "The accountants work carefully in getting out the final numbers."
- Weak: "We will give consideration to your idea."
- Stronger: "We will consider your idea."
- Weak: "The function of this office is the collection of accounts."
- Stronger: "This office collects accounts."

Other weak verb forms can also submerge the action.

- Weak: "Stabilization of the compound took place early in the experiment."
- Stronger: "The compound stabilized early in the experiment."

In the weak versions, the action has disappeared because the writer has turned the action verb into a noun.

Sometimes, using gerunds brings the action to the surface. (*Gerunds* are the noun/verb words ending in *-ing*.)

Submerged	**Surfaced**
by the use of the gerunds	by using gerunds
a resumption of operations will	resuming operations will
a reduction of costs can	reducing costs can

Note that each stronger or surfaced example is shorter than its weak or submerged counterpart.

TEST YOURSELF

BRINGING SUBMERGED VERBS TO THE SURFACE

Rewrite the following sentences. Change passive voice to active voice. Bring the submerged verbs to the surface. Say things as directly as you can. You'll find you can eliminate many words in the process.

1. These reports are concerned with the development of new safety measures.
2. He offered a proposed solution to the problem.
3. Mr. Huffman made payment today.
4. The employees gave recognition to I-Hsin for her persistence and hard work.
5. We are finally making progress toward our major goals.

6. The legislative subcommittee made a determination yesterday that our agency would continue to receive funding.
7. The auditors made a check of all expenditures from the past quarter.
8. Janet and Malik did an analysis of that report.
9. It is our recommendation that the agency make a distribution of nonperishable foods to the homeless.
10. After conducting a careful review of the evidence, the jury reached a decision to acquit the man.
11. These changes will make our process more streamlined.
12. The finalization of the contract occurred yesterday.

See the Appendix for answers.

WRITING TIP: SUBSTITUTE ACTION VERBS FOR FORMS OF "TO BE"

Forms of "to be" ("am," "is," "are," "was," "were") have less energy and interest than action verbs do. Whenever possible, opt for action verbs.

- Less energy: "My boss *was* always a believer in empowerment."
- More energy: "My boss always *believed* in empowerment."

Trying to avoid forms of the verb "to be" might even force you to become creative and descriptive:

- Less energy: "After the office social, people were happier."
- More energy: "After the office party, people *smiled, chatted,* and *thanked* the members of the Social Committee."

CHOOSING YOUR WORDS: TONE IN WRITING

Tone reflects the way you sound on paper, the way you convey an attitude or mood. Just as spoken tone strongly affects your listener, tone in writing strongly affects your reader. When readers open a letter that is harsh or cold, they are certainly less likely to respond to your requests.

We might describe tone as friendly, indifferent, angry, personal, confident, matter-of-fact, or serious. Choose a tone that is appropriate to your particular reader, purpose, and subject matter.

The Right Tone

The appropriate tone for most business writing conveys friendliness, concern, and respect—without being overly familiar or ingratiating, and without hedging.

Business writing is becoming more informal, friendly, and straightforward. Nevertheless, an element of judgment is usually involved in finding the right tone. You need to judge, for example, when a personal expression is just right and when a reflection of your personality, opinions, and feelings would be distracting or embarrassing. You need to judge when you're being businesslike at the cost of being friendly.

In his book *Games People Play,* Eric Berne describes a concept known as transactional analysis.[3] According to this theory, the human personality is composed of three discrete elements called the *child,* the *parent,* and the *adult.* Any transaction, or contact between two people, is affected by the dominant element. The dominant element might be revealed in the tone of a memo or letter. For example, consider the following three statements:[4]

1. If the people in the office weren't so noisy, I could get my work done without having to stay late every night. [Whiny tone, blaming others, and playing for sympathy like a *child.*]

2. If you would just plan a little better, you could get your work done on time. [I-told-you-so, do-it-right tone that a *parent* might use with an errant child.]

3. I suggest you close your office door when there's a distraction so that you won't be disturbed. [Offers a reasonable solution to the problem and sounds very *adult.*]

Most people respond to reasonable, straightforward communication. When they are addressed as adults by adults, they react as adults should react. Keeping in mind the principles of transactional analysis, make sure your writing has an adult tone.

Ways to Find the Right Tone

Finding the right tone is not always easy, but it helps to think from the standpoint of your reader. Some methods for finding the right tone include:

- Use "you," "your," or "yours" to address your reader personally and add immediacy to your letter or report. One of the worst tone offenses in government writing is to refer to people as if they were inanimate objects. Notice the difference between the two sentences below:

  - The leg injury is disabling; therefore, the payee is entitled to benefits.

  - We found that you have a disabling leg injury; therefore, you are entitled to benefits.

  The two changes to the second sentence are the use of "you" and the active voice.

- Use "I" or, if you are writing on behalf of your organization, use "we." Let the reader know that a human is writing, not a machine.
  - I look forward to seeing you at the conference.
  - We'll let you know when we receive your application.
- Also use "I" to:
  - Write in a less negative or accusatory tone
  - Soften the blow of unpleasant news.

Figure 4-1 shows the contrast between statements using second person ("you") and those using first person ("I"). Note that the "I" statements are wordier. Sometimes you must use more words to convey the accurate meaning and the appropriate tone.

Figure 4-1 ◆ Using Second and First Person

Second Person "You"	First Person "I"
You didn't write the memo in the correct format.	I'd like to spend some time with you going over our correspondence formats.
You were late coming back from lunch at 2:30 p.m.	I want to clarify our lunch-period policy. You must take your 30-minute lunch period between 11:30 a.m. and 2:00 p.m. We need everyone back at work by 2:00 p.m.

Second Person "You"	First Person "I"
You must resubmit your request using the right form.	I can expedite your refund, so I'm enclosing Form 112E. Please fill it out, sign your full name on line 5, and return the form to me.
You miscalculated the total cost, and you owe us $243.	I recalculated the cost of your purchase based on the changes you requested. The total cost is now $943. I credited your deposit of $700 to your account, so the balance due to us is $243.
You can't bring the class for a ride on NASA's shuttle.	Though I'm sorry we can't give shuttle rides to your class, I'm enclosing a simulation video I'm sure they'll enjoy. I'm also sending along Space Camp applications for everyone.

- *Say "please," "thanks," and "thank you"* where appropriate.
  - "Please fill out the form so we can send you the reimbursement check."
  - "Thank you for letting us know your change of address."
- *Ask questions.*
  - "Would you like to have this delivered earlier than Wednesday?"

- "Have we left any questions unanswered?"
- "May we have your reply by November 13?"

- *Use italics,* ALL CAPS, or ***bold*** type sparingly to emphasize points.

- *Use exclamation points with much restraint* in business writing.

- *Use a sympathetic tone only when appropriate.* For instance, if you are writing to a widow who is asking questions about benefits, you might want to start the letter by saying: "We are sorry to hear about the death of your husband." If, however, this is the fourth letter you have sent to the same widow, don't just add the same line by rote.[5]

- When you have to communicate bad news or a disappointing response, try to put yourself in the reader's place. Try to *convey friendliness, concern, and warmth.* Or try to defuse the situation. Don't argue with the reader—just supply the information needed to clarify points that might be confusing or misleading.
  - Instead of: "You are not qualified for this benefit."
  - Try: "Unfortunately, you do not qualify for this benefit."

- *Use "must" to indicate requirements.* The word "must" is the clearest way to convey to your readers what they have to do. Avoid using "shall" or "should."
  - "The governor must approve it."
- If you're saying no and asking for a response, be sure to *state the benefits of responding.*
  - "We will process your order as soon as we receive your check."
- If you're writing to complain, state facts and avoid emotion—which is not easy to do when you're angry. Probably the most effective approach is to *be firm and specific while keeping a sense of humor.*
- *If an apology is called for, make it*—without groveling or hedging. Apologize at once, for something specific, in as few words as possible.
  - Instead of: "Rest assured that we deeply regret the inconvenience our error has possibly caused you."
  - Try: "Thanks for informing us of the error. We hope it has not inconvenienced you."
- Where appropriate, *end on a positive note* by mentioning corrective action.

– "We're sending the balance of your refund today."

- Sometimes you need to qualify a statement; in those cases, words like "apparently" and "in general" are appropriate. But if you use such words habitually, your writing will have a hedging tone and imply that you aren't quite sure about what you're saying. *Here are some qualifying words and phrases to watch out for:*

  - apparently
  - in general
  - ordinarily
  - as a rule
  - in many instances
  - seems to indicate
  - as a usual case
  - in most cases
  - seemingly
  - commonly
  - it appears
  - usually
  - generally
  - normally

- *Use neutral or positive language* that puts the situation in the best light.

  – Instead of: "Because you failed to set up a team meeting, we must postpone the next phase of the ABC Project."

  – Try: "We will proceed with the next phase of the ABC Project after you set up a team meeting."

- *When you can convey good news, make it sound good.*
  - Instead of: "This letter will inform you that you will be sponsored as this staff's representative to the annual meeting."
  - Try: "Congratulations! Staff members have chosen you to represent them at the annual meeting."
- *Be sincere.* Don't gush. Don't lead the reader to question your credibility.
  - Instead of: "The response was fantastic."
  - Try: "Your idea received overwhelming support. The managers voted to feature it at the next staff meeting."
- *Don't make it seem as if you're talking down to your reader.*
  - Instead of: "You realize, obviously, that those results couldn't possibly be valid. It is well known, of course, that . . ."
  - Try: "These results may not be valid."

TEST YOURSELF

IMPROVING YOUR TONE

Rewrite these lines to give them a friendlier, more confident tone.

1. The proposed high-speed boats, though not as fast as those of other agencies, will have ample speed for a lot of suspect chases.
2. The regulatory program will protect the public from greedy companies that place profits ahead of service to consumers.
3. If there is anything you don't understand, you may call me as long as it's not after business hours.
4. Because you failed to sign the application, we cannot proceed.
5. We have a new time-keeping policy that you should be aware of and pay attention to.
6. This software program usually helps accountants complete their tasks on time. Our beta testing seems to indicate that, in most cases, monthly reports were out on time or generally within a few days of the deadline. Apparently, this is an improvement over what was commonly seen in the past.
7. You might not have read these steps in the manual, but it would be a good idea for you to follow them if you know what's good for you.
8. Your request for the balance of your benefit check has been received by this office and is being taken care of.
9. Unfortunately, you sent our visitors to the wrong building and Kate had to interrupt her work to go escort them to the customer service office.
10. I must have you review and sign off immediately on the enclosed personnel handbook.

See the Appendix for suggested answers.

Voice and tone can either strengthen or weaken the impact of writing. Using the active voice, selecting strong verbs, and deciding on the appropriate tone can make a world of difference in your writing.

In an active sentence, the person or agency performing an action is the subject of the sentence, whereas in a passive sentence the person or item acted upon is the subject of the sentence. Although you might have occasion to use the passive voice, using the active voice in most of your writing will make your sentences sound more natural, direct, clear, and confident.

Make your writing stronger by selecting strong verbs. Use the verb "to be" only when necessary and avoid submerged verbs—those combined with auxiliary or other weak verbs and turned into nouns.

Finally, choose a tone that is both professional and friendly, and appropriate to your reader, your purpose, and the subject matter. To convey a friendly tone, use "you," "we," and "I" whenever possible. Use "must" for requirements, and whether conveying good or bad news, keep your message sincere and positive. Use qualifying words and phrases sparingly, and make your apologies brief and specific.

NOTES

1 William Zinsser, *On Writing Well: The Classic Guide to Writing Nonfiction*, 7th ed. (New York: HarperCollins, 2006), 67.
2 Plain Language Action and Information Network, "Writing User-Friendly Documents." Online at http://www.plainlanguage.gov (accessed January 2008).
3 Eric Berne, *Games People Play* (New York: Grove Press, 1964).
4 Ibid.
5 Plain Language Action and Information Network, "Use a Sympathetic Opening." Online at http://www.plainlanguage.gov (accessed March 14, 2007).

CHAPTER 5

Editing: Writing with Clarity and Conciseness

◆ **Jargon and Gobbledygook** ◆

Because Maria had done such a good job with her first writing assignment, her supervisor asked her to continue reviewing the writing of others—mainly staff—on a regular basis. She found that the documents she was reviewing tended to have long and often confusing sentences. The writers tended to favor outdated expressions, such as "enclosed please find" and "we are in receipt of your application." They also used cumbersome phrases, such as "we deem it advisable" or "we will endeavor to ascertain." Maria found pretentious words like "promulgate" and "reside" sprinkled throughout the documents. Her goal was to make the letters and reports as clear and reader-friendly as possible.

When you edit your work, you want to make sure that your message is crystal clear and to the point. Your reader should not have to muddle through confusing, excess verbiage to discover the meaning. Readers who become frustrated by unclear writing might not read a document at all. What's the point of a regulation if the people it affects don't—or can't—read it? And what are the odds that people will comply with a regulation if they can't understand it?

HOW TO IMPROVE CLARITY

You can make your writing briefer and clearer. To reduce the number of words in your document, use short sentences, create lists whenever possible, replace wordy expressions, relax old-fashioned grammar rules, avoid cumbersome phrases, delete redundancies, use shorter words when possible, and use parallelism.

Use Short Sentences

Many documents are never read or understood because of long, confusing sentences. Short sentences:

- Show clear thinking
- Break information into small, easy-to-process units
- Add vigor and clarity to your documents

- Help you translate complicated provisions into understandable language
- Hold the reader's interest

The following is an example of a complex sentence that was divided into four shorter, clearer sentences:

Before	After
For good reasons, the Secretary may grant extensions of time in 30-day increments for filing of the lease and all required bonds, provided that additional extension requests are submitted and approved before the expiration of the original 30 days or the previously granted extension.	We may extend the time you have to file the lease and required bonds. Each extension will be granted for a 30-day period. To get an extension, you must write to us, giving the reason that you need more time. We must receive your extension request in time to approve it before your current deadline or extension expires.

In the following example, the "if" clause was made into a separate sentence:

Before	After
If you take less than your entitled share of production for any month, but you pay royalties on the full volume of your entitled share in accordance with the provisions of this section, you will owe no additional royalty for that lease of prior periods when you later take more than your entitled share to balance your account. This also applies when the other participants pay you money to balance your account.	Suppose that one month you pay royalties on your full share of production but take less than your entitled share. In this case, you may balance your account in one of the following ways without having to pay more royalty: (a) take more than your entitled share in the future, or (b) accept money from other participants.

Note that in the example above, the writer began the first sentence with "suppose that" and the second sentence with "in this case" to preserve the relationship between the two sentences.[1]

Sometimes we try to pile up ideas or verbs in a single sentence. This confuses the reader. Try to include only one or two ideas in each sentence. Padraic Spence, author of *Write Smart: The Complete Guide to Business Writing,*[2] gives the following example of a long sentence and its revision. The same six verbs appear in boldface for each version.

Before	After
We **recommend** the Systems Development Division **prepare** a machine-checking program for the Exhibit 550 as soon as possible since this program **can save** time for the division, and because it **will advance** the dates by which finished output reports **can be** available, we **should assign** the project priority over all other projects.	We **recommend** the System Development Division **prepare** a machine-checking program for the Exhibit 550 as soon as possible. This program **can save** time for the division and **advance** the dates by which finished output reports **can be** available. Therefore, we **should assign** the project priority over all other projects.

Divide Material into a List

If you have a complex paragraph with several parts, you can help your reader by dividing the parts into a list. A numbered or bulleted list will help your reader locate the information more easily and focus on each idea separately.

Vertical lists:

- Highlight levels of importance
- Help the reader understand the order in which things happen
- Make it easy for the reader to identify all necessary steps in a process
- Add blank space for easy reading
- Are an ideal way to present items, conditions, and exceptions

Two examples from the PLAIN website follow:[3]

Before	After
Each completed well drilling application must contain a detailed statement including the following information: the depth of the well, the casing and cementing program, the circulation media (mud, air, foam, etc.), the expected depth and thickness of freshwater zones, and well site layout and design.	With your application for a drilling permit, provide the following information: • Depth of the well • Casing and cementing program • Circulation media (mud, air, foam, etc.) • Expected depth and thickness of freshwater zones • Well site layout and design

Before	After
If a deponent fails to answer a question propounded, or a party upon whom a request is made under § 4.70, or a party on whom interrogatories are served fails to adequately respond or objects to the request, or any part thereof, or fails to permit inspection as requested, the discovering party may move the administrative law judge for an order compelling a response or inspection in accordance with the request.	You may move the administrative law judge for an order compelling a response or inspection if: • A deponent fails to answer a question; • A party upon whom you made a request under § 4.70 or a party on whom you served interrogatories does not adequately respond or objects to the request; or • A party on whom you made a request under § 4.70 or a party on whom interrogatories are served does not permit inspection as requested.

Be careful not to overuse vertical lists. Use them to highlight important information, not to overemphasize trivial matters. If you use bullets, use square or round ones. Large, creative bullets with strange shapes tend to distract the reader.

Replace Wordy Expressions

Many of the expressions below were once considered standard business English. Several are standard legal expressions. Today they sound stiff, stale, or pompous.

The times change, and business English changes with them. We're more relaxed in our ways of dressing and speaking and living our lives; we can relax more in our writing, too. Even lawyers are realizing that they can write plainly and still be precise and accurate. Joseph Kimble has commented on this issue:

> *Plain language is more precise than traditional legal and official language—I hesitate to say legalese and officialese—because plain language lays bare all the ambiguities, inconsistencies, uncertainties, and mistakes that traditional style, with all its excesses, tends to cover up.*[4]

The following list shows how to update some worn-out expressions. The left column contains old business writing standards that now sound out of place. The right column suggests alternatives. Many of the alternatives will improve your style and prevent confusion.

Instead of	Try
aforementioned (questionnaire)	omit; or say "the questionnaire I mentioned earlier"
allow me to point out; permit me to point out	please note
are in receipt of	received
as per your request	regarding your request
at an early date	soon; by (exact date)
at this time; at this point in time; at the present time	now
at this writing; as of this writing	omit; when else could it be? or say "now"

Instead of	Try
avail yourself of the opportunity	omit; or say "find time to" or "get the chance"
at your earliest convenience	omit; or say "as soon as you can" or "by (specific date)"
be of service to you	serve you; help you
contents noted	omit
desirous of	wish to
during such time as	when, while
enclosed please find/attached please find	see the copy I've enclosed; the enclosed copy shows
feel	unless you're expressing an emotion, use "think" or "believe"
for your information	omit
I have before me your letter	omit
I remain	omit
in a hasty manner	hastily; quickly
in compliance with your request	as you requested
a check in the amount of	a check for (amount); a (amount) check
in the event that	if
in the near future	specify when
kindly	please
legal terms: hereto, herewith, hereby, hereinafter, said, etc.	express in a simpler way (e.g., within, with this)
please be advised that	note that (or omit)

Instead of	Try
pursuant to your request; in reference to your request	refer to previous correspondence more directly (e.g., "we received your March 8th request")
recent date	specify date
referenced letter	the letter; the letter of (specified date)
regret to inform you	sorry to tell you
relative to	about
same (e.g., "we have cashed same")	Specify what "same" is (e.g., the check)
subject; employee	he; she
take the liberty of (telling you)	omit; or say, "we'd like to tell you"
take this opportunity to	omit; get to the subject
thanking you in advance	presumptuous; say, "if you will (action), I will appreciate it"
the writer(s)	I/we
the undersigned	I/we
this letter will acknowledge	omit; get to the point
trusting you will; trusting this is	omit; introduces doubt
under separate cover	in another envelope; in an express mail letter, etc.
we wish to state	we believe, we want to assure you

Relax Old-Fashioned Grammar Rules

Some of what we've been taught to think of as rules of grammar are really matters of usage; that is, of what is considered acceptable in using our language. Here are some rules that have now been relaxed or done away with:

- Don't use contractions in business writing. Today, using words like "it's," "don't," we're," and "here's" is seen as acceptable, and even advisable. These words help us cut through formality and make our writing friendly in tone.

- Never start a sentence with "and" or "but." Today, accepted English usage recognizes that starting a sentence with one of these words might be highly effective or quite weak. Writers are allowed to follow their instincts.

- Never end a sentence with a preposition. Current opinion says that this rule is one you don't have to rely on.

Avoid Cumbersome Phrases

Many writers think that using more words will give them a more elevated style or a style that is proper for business correspondence. They use phrases when a word will do; they use expressions that are roundabout rather than to the point. The result is writing that is officious, cumbersome, and often confusing—a chore to read.

- "Please be advised that, in the event of fire, employees should avail themselves of the opportunity to exit via . . ."

Some cumbersome expressions and suggested remedies follow.

Instead of	Try
adversely impact on	hurt
a large percentage of	many
a total of $250	$250
be in possession of	have
be of the opinion that	believe, think
despite the fact that	though
due to the fact that	due to, since, because
during which time	while
endeavor to ascertain	try to find out
exhibits a tendency to	tends to
for a period of a month	for a month
for the purpose of	to, for
give consideration to	consider
have occasion to be	have reason to be
has a requirement for	requires
in accordance with	by, following, under
in the majority of instances	often, usually
in the month of April	in April

Instead of	Try
in a number of cases	sometimes
in reference to	about
in the near future	soon
in the neighborhood of	about
in the field of economics	in economics
in view of the fact that	in view of, since
is authorized to	may
make an appearance	appear
not in a position	unable
on or before	by
range all the way from	range from
subsequent to	after
there are many people who think that	many people think
until such time	when
we deem it advisable	we suggest
with a view to	to
with regard to	about
without further delay	now

Delete Redundancies

Redundant writing repeats itself; it says, unintentionally, the same thing twice. Redundancies often creep in when we feel compelled to pad our business writing with filler phrases, such as those shown in parentheses below:

- "He was named (to the position of) director last week."
- "We hope to see you (at an) early (time)."
- "The man is unusual (in nature) but honest (in character)."

Sometimes redundancies emerge when, in trying to make things absolutely clear, we overdo it. It's all too easy to say:

- "After our boss reviewed the (important) essentials, she gave us an (unexpected) surprise."
- "We will hear the (final) outcome tonight."

The following are some common redundant expressions. The words in parentheses are unnecessary.

Noun Forms	Verb Forms	Adjective and Other Forms
(total) annihilation	appoint (to the position of)	adequate (enough)
(major) breakthrough	ascend (up)	big (in size)
capitol (building)	attach (together)	(entirely) complete
(fellow) colleague	climb (up)	contemporary (in time)
(final) completion	coalesce (together)	each (and every)
consensus (of opinion)	combine (together)	(all) finished

Noun Forms	Verb Forms	Adjective and Other Forms
(mutual) cooperation	commute (back and forth)	first (and foremost)
courthouse (building)	congregate (together)	(exact) identical
(general) custom	continue (on, still)	large (in stature)
(doctorate) degree	continue (to remain)	never (at any time)
(complete) destruction	cooperate (jointly)	(more) preferable
(baffling) dilemma	cover (over)	same (identical)
(sudden) eruption	depreciated (in value)	sufficient (enough)
(necessary) essential	descend (down)	(completely) unanimous
(passing) fad	eliminate (entirely)	unless (and until)
(basic) fundamentals	follow (after)	whether (or not)
(opening) gambit	gather (together)	
(free) gift	join (together)	
(past) history	may (possibly)	
(present) incumbent	merge (together)	
(new) innovation	name (as, to the position of)	
lawyer (by occupation)	penetrate (into)	
twelve o'clock (midnight)	(continue to) persist	
(personal) opinion	(pre) plan	
complete (monopoly)	prejudge (in advance)	
(final) outcome	recall (back)	
(fellow) partner	recur (again)	
(advance) planning	revert (back)	

Noun Forms	Verb Forms	Adjective and Other Forms
(troublesome) predicament	skirt (around)	
(leading) protagonist	spell out (in detail)	
(original) prototype		
(temporary) reprieve		
(local) resident		
(end) result		

Sometimes we are repetitious in a different way: We use the same word or phrase over and over in the sentence or paragraph. Spence presents this example in a letter from his draft board:

> *A personal appearance before the appeal board may be requested if you are eligible to request an appeal to the appeal board. You may appeal to the appeal board without requesting a personal appearance before the appeal board, but if you wish to appear before the appeal board, you must specifically ask for the appearance in addition to requesting an appeal.*[5]

Use Shorter Words

Overblown words distract readers. Readers might end up paying more attention to how you're saying it than to what you're saying. And they might lose interest, especially if they have to look up words they don't know. Some inflated words and their deflated equivalents follow.

Instead of	Try
accompanied	went with
accomplished	done
activate	begin
advantageous	helpful
aggregate	total
ameliorate	improve
approximately	about
ascertain	find
assist	help
categorize	sort
commence	start
communicate	write, tell
construct	make
demonstrate	show
discontinue	stop
disseminate	give, issue, send
edifice	building
encounter	meet
endeavor	try
examination	test
expedite	hasten, hurry up
facilitate	ease, simplify
indicate	show
initial	first

Instead of	Try
initiate	begin
modification	change
promulgate	publish
procure	get, buy
reside	live
terminate	end, stop
utilize	use

TEST YOURSELF

FINDING A BETTER WAY TO SAY IT

Translate each of the following gobbledygook statements into relaxed, straightforward business English:

1. Due to the fact that we have had our security breached on several occasions during the period of the past year, we have initiated entirely new procedures to be followed during such times as we have guests congregate together for a tour.
2. Kindly commence a search of subject persons and eliminate entirely any undesirable contents of briefcases or handbags in their possession.
3. Disseminate badges to all guests and accompany them to the courthouse building first and foremost.
4. Pursuant to agency regulations, do not permit them in close proximity to sensitive material or allow them to be in possession of said material.

5. If a guest exhibits a tendency to wander into unauthorized areas or casts repeated glances at aforementioned material, we deem it desirable to congregate together each and every guest and exit in an expeditious manner.
6. We request your mutual cooperation in following according to the aforementioned regulations and herewith ensuring better and improved security for all.

See the Appendix for suggested answers.

TEST YOURSELF

DEFLATING WORDS

Replace each inflated word with a short word (or with two or three short words).

1. communicate	1.
2. component	2.
3. constitute	3.
4. necessitate	4.
5. depart	5.
6. magnitude	6.
7. convene	7.
8. exhibit (verb)	8.
9. equitable	9.
10. transmit	10.

See the Appendix for suggested answers.

TEST YOURSELF

DEFLATING SENTENCES

To deflate these sentences, you'll have to interpret them. Rewrite each sentence to clarify its meaning; express the thought in an entirely different way if you like. Cut any unnecessary words. Whenever you can replace long words with short ones, or unfamiliar words with familiar ones, do so.

1. You will accelerate your career growth and attain a sizably increased income as you maximize your optimal attributes.
2. We deem inoperable your methodology for eliminating injurious behavioral patterns.
3. The established procedural practices cannot be adequately reconciled with maximum utilization of our human resources.
4. Radioactivity is presently an excessively dangerous possibility.
5. Because a majority of the students were inadequately prepared, their answers exhibited numerous inaccuracies.

See the Appendix for suggested answers.

TEST YOURSELF

AVOIDING REPETITION

Read the two examples of repetitious sentences below. Write a shorter, clearer version of each sentence.

A personal appearance before the appeal board may be requested if you are eligible to request an appeal to the appeal board.

When the process of freeing a vehicle that has been stuck results in ruts or holes, the operator will fill the rut or hole created by such activity before removing the vehicle from the immediate area.

See the Appendix for suggested answers.

Use Parallelism

Making the parts parallel means using the same grammatical construction and beginning with the same part of speech. Notice that, in the preceding sentence, we did not say, "Making the parts parallel means that you should use . . ." We said, "Making . . . means using . . ." The concept is this: Ideas that look roughly alike in your mind should look roughly alike on the page. In grammar, this is called *parallel construction*.

Dr. Martin Luther King, Jr., in his "I Have a Dream" speech, used both repetition and parallel construction effectively:

> *Now is the time to make real the promises of democracy. Now is the time to rise from the dark and desolate valley of segregation to the sunlit path of racial justice. Now is the time to open the doors of opportunity to all of God's children. Now is the time to lift our nation from the quicksands of racial injustice to the solid rock of brotherhood.*[6]

The following familiar phrases also illustrate the use of parallel construction:

- "One if by land, two if by sea."
- "Where there's a will, there's a way."
- "Saw sub, sank same."

- "Ask not what your country can do for you; ask what you can do for your country."

Even if you're uncertain of the grammar principles involved, you can usually detect nonparallel items by using your ear. Nonparallel passages sound awkward. Read the following statements:

Nonparallel	Parallel
The new copier is efficient, easy to operate, and it is relatively inexpensive.	The new copier is efficient, easy to operate, and relatively inexpensive.
The steel companies lost money because of high costs, foreign competition had increased, and they had inefficient processes.	The steel companies lost money because of high costs, increased foreign competition, and inefficient processes.
The trip will involve traveling by airplane, bus, and by car.	The trip will involve traveling by airplane, bus, and car.

Examples of Nonparallel Construction

There are specific ways to diagnose problems with parallelism, or to match the parts. Some common problems are:

- Using the wrong part of speech
  - Unmatched: "He acted quickly and with care."
  - Matched: "He acted quickly and carefully."

- Shifting from active to passive voice.
  - Unmatched: "The company finished the job on time, but many errors were made by its workers."
  - Matched: "The company finished the job on time, but its workers made many errors."
- Shifting person
  - Unmatched: "When you leave our building, take a left; then I usually go three blocks and take a right." (third person, first person)
  - Matched: "When you leave our building, take a left; then go three blocks and take a right." (second person, second person)

Presenting Lists in Parallel Form

Lists are much easier to read when the items they contain are parallel. In the list on the left, three of the items begin with adverbs (what, when, and where); two, with gerunds (getting, eating); and one, with a noun (passport). In the list on the right, each item begins with a noun.

Nonparallel	Parallel
◆ passport	◆ passport
◆ what to wear and pack	◆ clothing

- where to stay
- getting around the city
- when and where workshops meet
- eating out

- hotels
- transportation
- workshops
- restaurants

Reasons for Matching the Parts

Making the parts parallel is important because:

- It makes the passage shorter.
- It makes the passage clearer.
- It puts you, the writer, in a better light. If the parts of your statements are not matched, the reader might begin to doubt your attention to detail and even the logic of your thinking.

TEST YOURSELF

MAKING THE PARTS PARALLEL

A. Make the parts of this outline match.

1. Quality of classroom teaching
    a. How well the instructor knows the subject
    b. Ability to relate to students
    c. Answering questions well

2. How much the instructor has contributed to the university
3. Instructor's contributions to the community
   a. Volunteer work related to instructor's field of expertise
   b. What has been done outside the instructor's field
4. Instructor's publications: quality and quantity

B. Here is part of an outline for a presentation on the qualities of a successful manager. Tighten it by making the parts match.

- Ability to cope with stressful situations
- Being a good role model
- How to foster teamwork
- Communicate clearly at all levels
- Taking responsibility

C. Rewrite the following sentences to make the parts match.

1. The history course was stimulating and a challenge.
2. If you want to buy shares in Fund XYZ by mail, fill out and sign the account application form, making your check payable to "The XYZ Fund," and write your Social Security number on your check.
3. She signed up for a course in cake decorating and one in the design of watercolors.
4. I go golfing in the fall, in spring I like to play tennis, and my favorite sport in winter is skiing.
5. He couldn't decide whether to take the job or if he should go to graduate school as he had planned.

See the Appendix for suggested answers.

OTHER TIPS FOR WRITING MORE CLEARLY

Some simple guidelines will also help you make your writing clear:

- *If you use an acronym (abbreviation) your readers might not know, spell it out the first time you use it.* An example is "Department of Labor (DOL) contractors . . . ." In general, use abbreviations only to refer to terms that are central to the document. For example, if a regulation is about the Comprehensive Environmental Response, Compensation, and Liability Act, you can refer to it as CERCLA. Do not abbreviate terms you use only once or a few times. Write them out each time.

- *Use the same term consistently to identify a specific thought or object.* For example, if you use the term "senior citizens" to refer to a group, continue to use this term throughout your document. Do not substitute another term, such as "the elderly," that will make your reader wonder if you are referring to the same group.[7]

- *Use the simplest tense you can.* Use the present tense to avoid the clutter of compound verbs. A document written in the present tense is more immediate and forceful and less complicated. The following examples, which appear in *Writing User-Friendly Documents,* illustrate the use of simple tenses.[8]

Before	After
These sections describe types of information that would satisfy the application requirements of Circular A-110 as it would apply to this grant program.	These sections tell you how to meet the requirements of Circular A-110 for this grant program.
Applicants who were Federal employees at the time that the injury was sustained should have filed a compensation request at that time. Failure to do so could have an effect on the degree to which the applicant can be covered under this part.	You may not be covered under this part if: (a) You were a Federal employee at the time of the injury; and (b) You did not file a report with us at that time.

- *Avoid jargon whenever possible. Jargon* is the specialized vocabulary and idioms shared by those in the same organization, profession, etc. If a scientific, technical, or legal term is the best word to describe what you mean, use it. If you think your reader might be unfamiliar with the term, define it the first time you use it.
  - "Appellate litigation (lawsuits brought before a court of appeals) is conducted by attorneys in the national headquarters."

BEING PRECISE

Read the following paragraph:

Participants in the seminar said the curriculum related to the major responsibilities involved in their employment. They indicated that they had obtained information that would enable them to perform their obligations. One participant noted that the seminar design provided for concentration on certain areas for a given length of time.

Hard to grasp? Read it again.

Still not clear? The paragraph is a model of *imprecision.* You can't read it and get a clear picture of what happened at the seminar; all you can do is try to interpret its meaning.

Now read the following paragraph and compare it to the one you just read:

Nearly 85 percent of participants in the project management seminar said the curriculum covered the major responsibilities in their positions, including project planning, scheduling, and control. They said they had learned about calculating cost and schedule variances that would enable them to deal with unexpected changes in their projects. One participant noted that the seminar design provided for three hours of concentration in critical path scheduling.

The second paragraph gives much more specific information and is more persuasive. Precise words that give solid evidence help you convince the reader.

- Imprecise: "Please send me your response as soon as possible."

- Precise: "Please send me your response by close of business Tuesday, April 17."

In some kinds of writing, precision is a must. Those who write regulations, procedures, specifications, or technical instructions must include considerable detail. They must spell out exactly what is or is not to be done, and they must describe exceptions and variations. They must say exactly what is meant:

- Imprecise: "Your new office is much nicer than your old one."

- Precise: "Your new office is larger, better equipped, and more conveniently located than your old one."

- Imprecise: "He had a long commute to work."

- Precise: "He spent an hour and a half commuting to work each day."

- Imprecise: "The children responded well to the teacher's presentation."

- Precise: "The children were quiet and attentive during the teacher's presentation, and they asked several thoughtful questions afterward."

The challenge in writing that requires much detail and great exactness is to be both precise and readable. Sometimes, you must make tradeoffs.

Identify Your Audience Precisely

When you're writing about requirements, use singular nouns and verbs to prevent confusion about whether a requirement applies to individual readers or to groups.

- Imprecise: "Individuals and organizations wishing to apply must file applications with the appropriate offices in a timely manner."
- Precise: "You must apply at least 30 days before you need the certification:
  - (a) If you are an individual, apply at the State office in the State where you reside.
  - (b) If you are an organization, apply at the State office in the State where your headquarters is located."

TEST YOURSELF

PAINTING A CLEAR PICTURE

Read the following statements.

Now read into them. Use your imagination.

Replace each statement with one that is specific. Make it interesting and informative. Write more than one sentence if you like.

1. The report related to recent events.
2. The weather was bad.
3. You must check the system frequently.
4. She spent a long time working on the presentation.
5. The boss liked your idea.
6. I plan to change jobs soon.

See the Appendix for suggested answers.

AVOIDING COMMON BARRIERS TO UNDERSTANDING

It's always a good idea to read over what you've written—out loud or to your mind's ear. Put yourself in the reader's place. How do you sound? Clear, forceful, and lively? Sure of yourself? Firm but friendly? Intelligent but not arrogant?

Also be aware of the words as they roll off your tongue. Is the flow smooth? Or do you stumble in places? Are there some almost unpronounceable patches? Does the rhythm tend to fall flat?

The following are suggestions for diagnosing and remedying some of the common barriers.

Watch Out for "Noun Sandwiches"

Sometimes, the rule about being concise must be broken. The following group of words would trip up most readers:

- "underground mine worker safety procedures development"

The tight knot of thoughts (noun sandwich) needs to be loosened by adding prepositions and articles to clarify relationships among the words:

- "development of safety procedures for the protection of workers in underground mines"

Place Words Carefully within Your Sentences

Keep subjects and objects close to their verbs. The following sentence is both long and poorly constructed:

- "The project leader, after hearing all the results of the annual evaluation and weighing the pros and cons of the evaluation team's recommendations, decided to make five major changes in the program."

By the time the readers get to the verb "decided," they might have forgotten that the subject is "project leader." Try this:

- "After hearing all the results of the annual evaluation and weighing the pros and cons of the evaluation team's recommendations, the project leader decided to make five major changes in the program."

Better still, put the ideas into two short sentences.

- "The project leader heard the results of the annual evaluation and weighed the pros and cons of the evaluation team's recommendations. He then decided to make five major changes in the program."

In this example from *Writing User-Friendly Documents*, it is difficult in the original version (the left column) to figure out which words relate to the forest products, which relate to the tribe, and which relate to the payments:[9]

Original	Modified
Upon the request of an Indian tribe, the Secretary may provide that the purchaser of the forest products of such tribe, which are harvested under a timber sale contract, permit, or other harvest sale document, make advance deposits, or direct payments of the gross proceeds of such forest products, less any amounts segregated as forest management deductions pursuant to section 163.25, into accounts designated by such Indian tribe.	If you ask us, we will require purchasers of your forest products to deposit their payment into an account that you designate. (a) You can instruct us to deposit advance payments, as well as direct payments, into the account. (b) We will withhold from the deposit any forest management deductions under section 163.25.

Put conditionals like "only" or "always" and other modifiers next to the words they modify.

- Ambiguous: "You are only required to provide the following."
- Clear: "You are required to provide only the following."

Avoid Ambiguous Phrasing

Avoid ambiguous phrasing, which can confuse your reader. The following is an example of such a phrase. The reader might have to read the statement several times to figure out that it doesn't mean "If you really want to have a disability . . . ."

- Ambiguous: "If you are determined to have a disability, we will pay you the following:"
- Clear: "If we determine that you have a disability, we will pay you the following:"

Make Pronoun References Clear

Have you cleared up any questions about which words your pronouns stand for? (In grammatical terms: Have you cleared up any faulty references?)

- Ambiguous: "The agencies have a number of field offices. Most of the work is done in them."
- Clear: "The agencies have a number of field offices. Most of the work is done in these offices."

Correct Dangling Modifiers

Have you made sure there are no dangling modifiers to confuse (or amuse) the reader?

- Dangling: "Here are some tips for protecting your valuables from our security staff."

Members of the security staff are not stealing valuables. They are offering tips.

- Clear: "Here are some tips from our security staff for protecting your valuables."

- Dangling: "After waiting 10 minutes, the engineer told us the elevator was not working."

The engineer did not wait 10 minutes. You did.

- Clear: "After we'd waited 10 minutes, the engineer told us the elevator was not working."

Use Words Correctly—Especially Similar Words

When you're concentrating on getting your thoughts down, it's easy to write one word when you mean another. It's also easy to use words carelessly, letting them slip by even though you're not sure that they're correct in the context.

Many errors are made because we mistake words that look and sound alike:

- assure/ensure/insure

- flout/flaunt

- effect/affect

- site/sight/cite

These errors can be embarrassing—but at least readers often understand despite them and give us credit for what we meant to say. Sometimes, however, the misuse of words can mislead or perplex:

- "The idea literally blew them away." (Really? Or did it figuratively blow them away?)
- "We will not stand for the prosecution (persecution?) of the handicapped."

CHECKING YOUR READABILITY

A document's *readability* is the level of difficulty at which it is written, and therefore the level of education required to understand it. Readability is based on:

- The average length of sentences
- The average number of syllables in a word

Readability of Familiar Publications[10]	
The Atlantic Monthly	Grade 12 (difficult)
The Wall Street Journal	Grade 11
The New York Times	Grade 10
Los Angeles Times	Grade 10
Business Week	Grade 10
Time magazine	Grade 10

Reader's Digest	Grade 8
Boston Globe	Grade 8
U.S.A. Today	Grade 7
People magazine	Grade 6 (easy)

A document with long sentences and many syllables is considered more difficult to read than one with shorter sentences and fewer syllables. A ninth-grade level is about the right level for most business documents. This level uses few long words and keeps sentences to about 15 words in length.

Computer programs, readability graphs, and "Fog" indexes are some of the ways to determine a document's readability. You can calculate the Fog index as follows:[11]

> *1. Find the average number of words per sentence. Use a sample of at least 100 words. Divide the total number of words by the number of sentences. This gives you the average sentence length.*
>
> *2. Count the number of words of three syllables or more per 100 words. Don't count (a) words that are capitalized; (b) combinations of short, easy words like bookkeeper; and (c) verbs that are made three syllables by adding "ed" or "es"—like "created" or "trespasses."*
>
> *3. Add the two figures above and multiply by 0.4. This will give you the Fog index. It corresponds roughly with the number of years of schooling a person requires to read a passage with ease and understanding.*

TEST YOURSELF

USING A FOG INDEX

Calculate and compare the Fog index of two writing samples—yours or someone else's.

1. Which sample was easier to read?
2. How could you improve either or both of the samples?

The essence of plain language is clarity. Documents written in plain language are much more likely to be read, understood, and heeded—in much less time. Plain language means:

- Using shorter sentences
- Scrapping business English relics, including legal expressions
- Avoiding cumbersome phrases
- Eliminating redundancies
- Making parts (words, phrases, and items in a list) parallel
- Minimizing and explaining acronyms and jargon
- Avoiding confusing words and phrases, such as noun sandwiches, dangling modifiers, ambiguous phrasing, and unclear pronoun references
- Placing words carefully within your sentence
- Using words correctly, especially those that look or sound alike

- Using simple tenses
- Using terms consistently

Although brevity is usually preferable in writing, sometimes you must use more words to convey a more precise meaning. Make sure your reader gets a clear, convincing picture of what you mean.

You can get an idea how readable your documents are by using a Fog index, which is based on sentence and word length. Although these aren't the only determiners of plain writing, they are important.

NOTES

1 Plain Language Action and Information Network, "Break Your Material Into Short Sentences." Online at http://www.plainlanguage.gov (accessed April 4, 2007).
2 Padraic Spence, *Write Smart: The Complete Guide to Business Writing* (Great Barrington, MA: North River Press, 1996), 96. Used with permission.
3 Plain Language Action and Information Network, "Use Lots of Lists." Online at http://www.plainlanguage.gov (accessed January 8, 2008).
4 Joseph Kimble, "Testifying to Plain Language," testimony before the House Subcommittee on Regulatory Affairs, March 1, 2006, *Michigan Bar Journal* (June 2006): 45.
5 *Write Smart,* 7. Used with permission.
6 Martin Luther King, Jr., "The I Have a Dream Speech." Online at http://www.usconstitution.net/dream.html (accessed April 12, 2007).
7 Plain Language Action and Information Network, "Use the Same Term Consistently for a Specific Thought or Object." Online at http://www.plainlanguage.gov (accessed January 8, 2008).

8 Plain Language Action and Information Network, "Use the Simplest Form of a Verb." Online at http://www.plainlanguage.gov (accessed January 8, 2008).
9 Plain Language Action and Information Network, "Place Words Carefully." Online at http://www.plainlanguage.gov (accessed January 8, 2008).
10 Deborah Dumaine, *Write to the Top: Writing for Corporate Success* (New York: Random House, 1989).
11 Robert Gunning, *The Technique of Clear Writing* (New York: McGraw-Hill, 1968).

CHAPTER 6

Adding Visual Impact to Your Writing

◆ How Does Your Document Look? ◆

Jon was working on a report for his boss's presentation before a congressional subcommittee. He had carefully planned and organized the report, drafted the paragraphs with topic sentences, checked for the proper tone, used the active voice, and performed a substantive edit to make sure the report was complete but not wordy. Still, something did not seem right.

"It's boring to look at," Jon decided. "I need to add more white space, more headings, and more graphics."

To add white space, Jon increased the margins on all sides, added space between sections of the report, and made bulleted or numbered lists wherever he could. He also added headings for the sections of the report.

Then he reread the document and thought about where graphics would be useful. "I don't want to just throw them in for decoration," he thought. He decided to use a line graph to show the effect of budget cuts on his agency's public information office. To illustrate how the office budgeted its time, he designed a pie chart with slices showing the different office functions. A flow chart showed the route of information from the agency to the public. When he was done, Jon stepped back and looked at his document again.

"That's much better," he thought. "Now someone might actually *want* to read it."

In writing government documents, you want your readers to get information, comply with requirements, and apply for benefits with the least amount of effort. To help your readers understand what you're writing, you need to create visually appealing documents.

John V. Thill and Courtland L. Bovée describe the benefits of carefully crafted visuals in business documents:

> *Well-designed visuals can bring your messages to life and help you connect to your audiences at both the intellectual and emotional levels. Visuals enhance the communication power of textual messages, and they can often convey some message points (such as spatial relationships and procedures) more effectively and more efficiently than words. . . . Busy readers often jump to visuals to try to get the gist of a message, and attractive visuals can draw readers deeper into your reports and presentations.*[1]

In this chapter, we will discuss how you can use these ideas to make your documents more visually appealing.

PLAIN LANGUAGE GUIDELINES FOR VISUAL FORMATTING

You can use appealing visual format to draw your readers' attention to information they need to know. Modify the layout and typography of your documents to make them more visually attractive.

Layout

Margins

- Provide margins of 1¼ to 1½ inches on either side of your text.
- Use justified left, but ragged right text throughout.

Headings

- Use uppercase and lowercase, not all caps.
- Set in boldface.
- Justify to the left margin.
- Triple-space before headings and double-space after (19.2 points before, 8.4 points after).

Typography

Fonts

- Use a proportionally spaced typeface like this one—rather than one in which all the letters have the same space, as in this example of `Courier` font.
- Avoid small, sans serif typefaces like this, which are difficult to read. Instead, select a larger serif font like this one.
- Don't mix fonts *within the text.*

Shading/Boxing

- Use shading and boxing only to accent graphs, charts, etc.

Bullets

- Use standard bullets. If you select others, such as diamonds or arrows, be consistent.
- Generally, don't use more than two types of bullets in a document.
- Use bullets instead of numbers except when you are presenting a sequence.

Bold/Italic/Underlining

- Use **bold** or *italic* for emphasis.
- Use italic for parenthetical information, like citations of laws.

Before You Finish

- Take a long look at the appearance of the document for eye appeal.
- Be sure the document is not visually confusing.
- Don't overuse layout and typographical devices.
- Check for odd shapes (like the "hourglass effect") that might have been created unintentionally as you composed the letter.

An Example of Plain Language Applied Visually

Below is a written message regarding rollover risk in some cars. Following it is a graphic used to convey the same idea.[2]

Before:

This is a multipurpose passenger vehicle which will handle and maneuver differently from an ordinary passenger car, in driving conditions which may occur on streets and highways and off road. As with other vehicles of this type, if you make sharp turns or abrupt maneuvers, the vehicle may roll over or may go out of control and crash. You should read driving guidelines and instructions in the Owner's Manual, and WEAR SEAT BELTS AT ALL TIMES.

After:

ENHANCING THE TEXT WITH GRAPHICS

When you have many facts, the best way to present them is often with a table, graph, chart, or illustration. When you're discussing a lot of data, one table or figure can be clearer and more memorable than five pages of text. These visual aids help readers who are visual thinkers as well as those who have time only to skim.

When using graphics:

- Each of your figures and tables should have a *purpose*. Don't throw them in just to spice up your report.

- Each graphic should convey only *one main point*. First decide what point you want to make. Then choose the type of figure that can best represent the data and convey that point.

- Keep graphics *simple.* Cluttered and confusing tables and figures can be overwhelming.
- *Label* your graphics so the reader can clearly and easily see what each column of a table, axis of a graph, and wedge of a pie chart describes.
- Review each graphic to make sure it can *stand alone.* The reader should be able to understand it completely, *even if she or he has not read the text.* (Remember how many times *you* have flipped through a report, reading only the headings, graphs, and charts.)
- Each graphic should have a *caption.* The caption should do more than tell the reader what the graphic shows, e.g., "Homicide Rates of Industrialized Nations, 1960–1990." The caption should also summarize the main point you want the graphic to convey—the bottom line or reason you included it in the first place. These captions may be written in sentence form, e.g., "Since 1960, the U.S. homicide rate has been more than ten times that of any other industrialized nation."

Although visual aids can enhance writing, they should be used only as a supplement for information discussed in the text. Make sure that you refer to the visual aid in the text, using the following guidelines:

- Try to place a visual aid on the same page as the text in which it is discussed or on the following page—never on the page before the text in which it is discussed.
- Refer to its location in the text. For example, "The following table . . ." or "The table on the next page . . . ."
- If you decide to put your visual aid in a separate section, such as an appendix, note its location in the text.

TYPES OF VISUAL AIDS

Figure 6-1 illustrates some common types of visual aids and their uses.

Some examples of visual aids and tips for their use follow.

Photographs

Use photographs to:

- Record an event
- Show the shape and surface appearance of an object

Figure 6-1 ◆ Types of Visual Aids and Their Uses

Type of Visual Aid	What It Shows	How to Use It
Photograph	An exact image of the item's appearance	To show an item exactly as it looks
Line drawing	An artist's rendering of what something looks like	To show shape or detail, but also information about process or operation (for example, use arrows to indicate direction)
Cutaway diagram	The inside of an item, relative to the exterior	To show the insides of mechanisms, buildings, and structures
Exploded diagram	The different physical elements of a mechanism and the way they fit together	To show how to assemble or disassemble a mechanism
Map	An item's location relative to other items	To show an item's position and distance from other items, to help the reader locate the item
Flow chart	Stages of a process	To show the steps in a process and to guide the operator through alternatives
Schematic	Stages of a process and the layout of parts in that process	To show the steps in a process, and the physical layout of each step
Screen Shot	What appears on a computer screen at a given time.	To show specific aspects of an application or process.

Type of Visual Aid	What It Shows	How to Use It
Table	A large body of data	To show large amounts of detailed information; to display exact numbers; and to compare individual entries and categories
Line graph	The way one variable changes in relation to another	To show trends over time and to compare trends
Pie chart	Proportions and percentages	To show relative amounts of various segments of a whole population
Bar chart	Comparisons among quantities	To compare various items for a particular time or to show how one item changes over time

- Illustrate the development of a phenomenon over a period of time
- Show objects that are difficult to draw
- Show actual appearances where details, color, tones, and textures are important
- Prove something is real

To make the use of photographs effective:

- Remove any distracting details by zooming in or cropping the photograph.
- Draw attention to the subject through focus, angle, and lighting.
- Place a familiar object, such as a ruler, book, or person, near the object being photographed (to show relative size).
- Show depth through the use of lighting and focus.

Don't use a photograph to show a process where flow is involved.

Figure 6-2 ◆ Sample Photograph

Drawings

Use drawings to:

- Show the appearance of an object or scene without unnecessary detail
- Show views impossible to create through photography without destroying the subject in the process
- Show objects that do not yet exist
- Emphasize the significant part of a mechanism or its function
- Focus on relationships or details that a photograph can't capture

To make the use of drawings effective:

- Omit any details in the drawing that do not contribute to the point you are trying to make.
- Emphasize parts of the drawing that carry the most information, such as the outline.
- Show equipment and other objects from the point of view of the person who will use them.
- Draw different parts of a drawing in proportion to one another, unless you indicate that certain parts are enlarged.

- Place labels where necessary for comprehension.
- Select the type of drawing to match the audience, such as:
  - – Cutaways for general audience
  - – Exploded views for mechanics
  - – Cross sections for engineers

Figures 6-3 through 6-5 give examples of how to use drawings as visual aids:

Figure 6-3 ◆ Sample Line Drawing

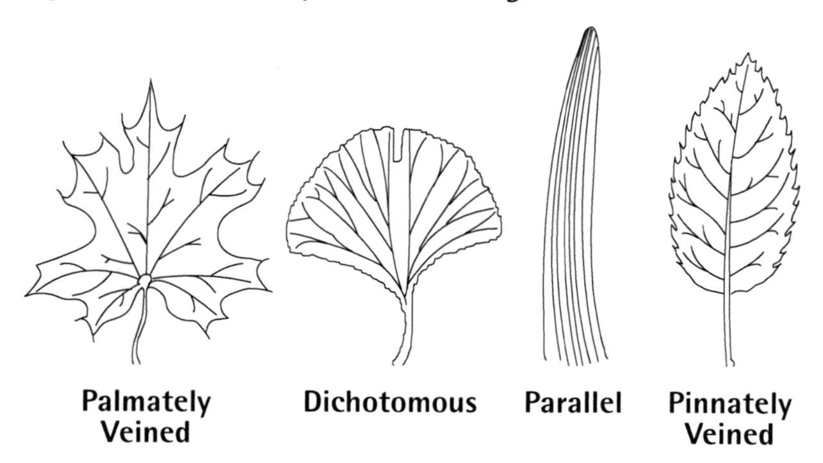

Figure 6-4 ◆ Sample Cutaway Diagram

Figure 6-5 ◆ Sample Exploded Diagram

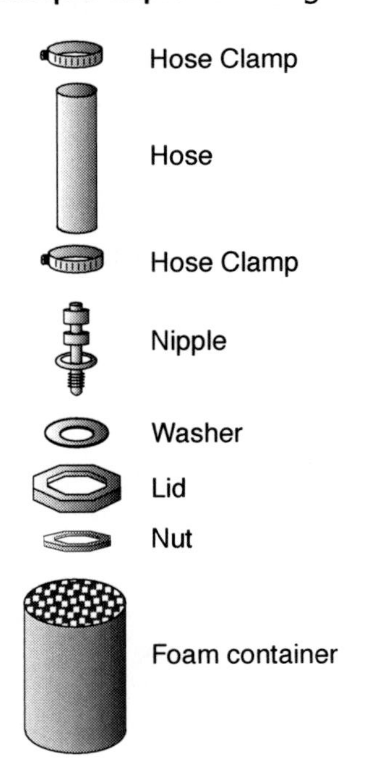

Maps

Use maps to show:

- Where things are located in relation to each other and to the reader's current location
- Geographical distribution of data or objects
- A complicated system or terrain

To make the use of maps effective:

- Keep maps simple; display only necessary details.
- Use obvious or familiar symbols.
- Follow natural color conventions (e.g., using blue for water).
- Simplify the display when possible without distorting crucial relationships.
- Include a display and a full legend.

Figure 6-6 gives an example of how to use maps effectively.

Figure 6-6 ◆ Sample Map

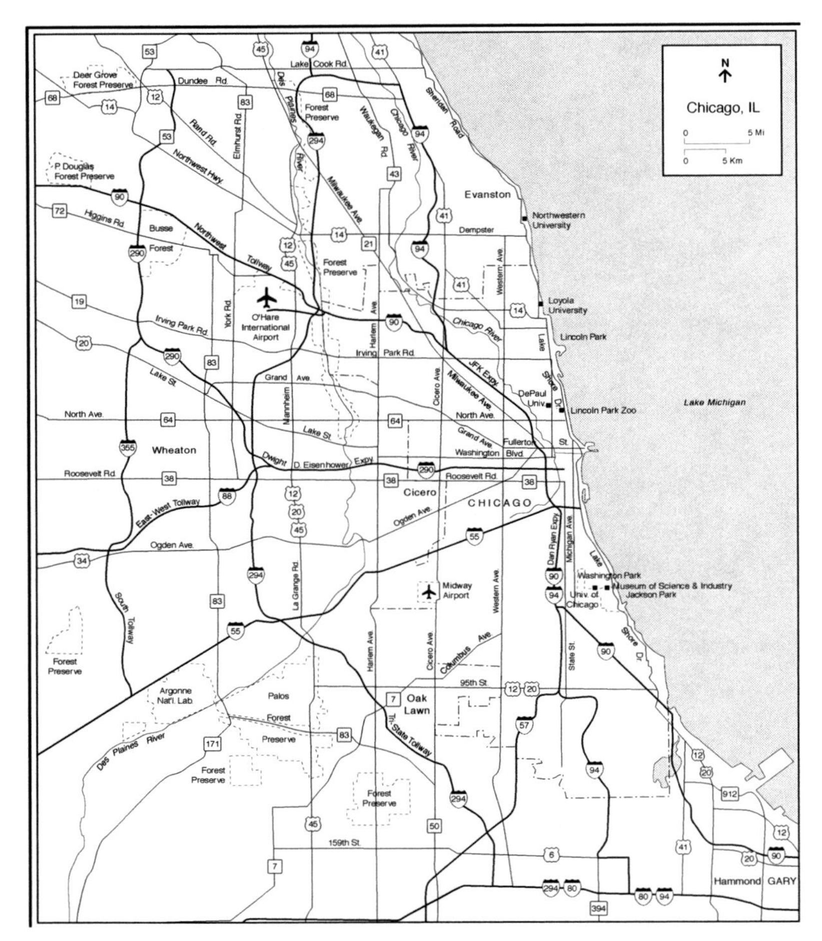

Flow Charts

Use flow charts to show:

- Stages in a process

- Sequence of steps in a procedure from beginning to end
- Interrelationships among the stages in a process

Flow charts are diagrams that show the stages in a process, indicating the sequence in which the stages occur (see Figure 6-7). Flow charts consist of arrows to indicate flow and icons to represent each stage in the process. Icons might include:

- Labeled blocks
- Pictorial representations
- Standardized symbols
  - Circles or oblongs to indicate starts and stops
  - Squares or rectangles to indicate actions
  - Diamonds to indicate stages at which the performer must make a decision
  - Hexagons to indicate stages at which the performer must make a check

When using flow charts:

- Make the flow from left to right or top to bottom.
- Label each stage.

- Include a key for symbols your readers might not understand.

Figure 6-7 ◆ Sample Flow Chart

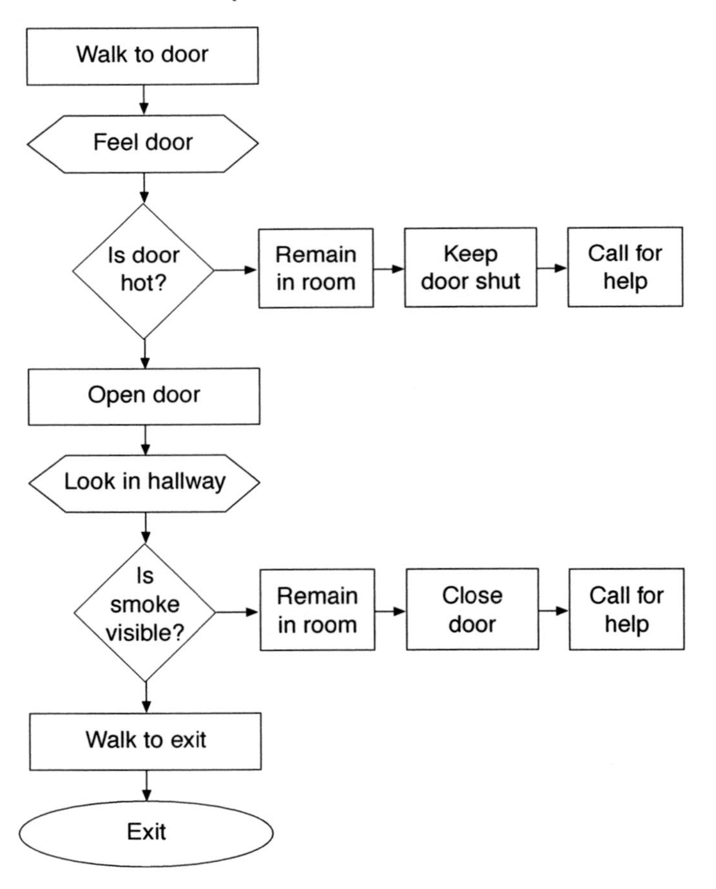

Schematics

Schematic diagrams are used primarily in electronics, chemistry, and electrical and mechanical engineering (see Figure 6-8). Use them to:

- Show an operation with lines and symbols rather than a physical likeness
- Emphasize the relationships among the parts at the expense of precise proportions

To make the use of schematics effective:

- Make clear in the text why the schematic is included.
- Include only necessary information.
- Keep terminology and abbreviations consistent.
- Position labels horizontally for ease of reading, if possible.
- Consider your reader's ability to understand the symbols in your schematic. (Symbols and their meanings are like a foreign language.)

Figure 6-8 ◆ Sample Schematic

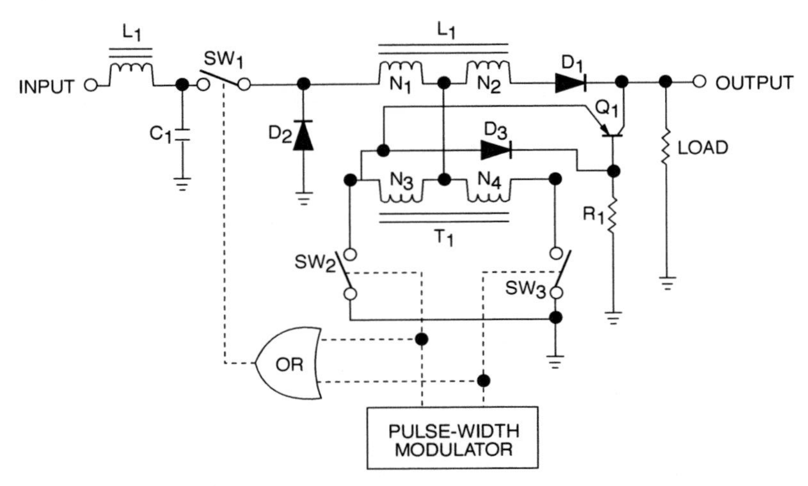

Modulated voltage regulator

Screen Shots

Screen shots, sometimes called screen captures, are bit-mapped graphics created by capturing what appears on the computer screen at a given time (see Figure 6-9). They are most often used to illustrate specific aspects of an application or process and are therefore the most common type of illustration found in computer books.

Screen shots are important to most paper manuals dealing with the use of systems, especially since we often use paper manuals away from the computer. The screen shots turn paper-based manuals into useful learning tools and make the text more appealing.

For difficult procedures, use more screen shots; for easier procedures, fewer. For basic instructions, such as how to navigate or perform basic operations, include screen shots to illustrate each step. For specific procedures, use an initial screen shot to indicate the "arrival state." This confirms to the users that they are starting from the right place. Use additional shots for each major screen transition.

Figure 6-9 ◆ Sample Screen Shot

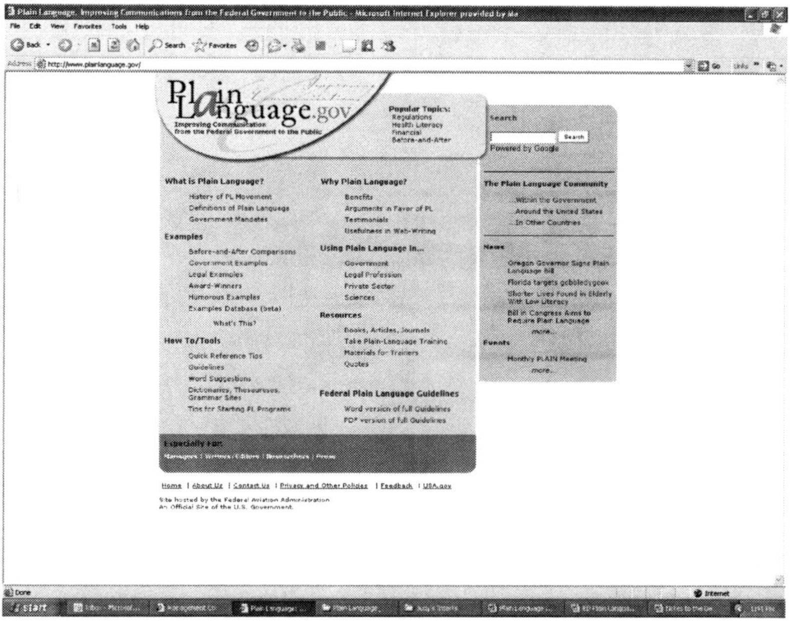

Some tips for using screen shots include:

- As with all visuals, use a caption below each screen shot and include a cross-reference in the text so the reader knows what step the screen shot relates to.

- When needed, insert a text box, circled area, or arrow on the screen shot to reinforce the instruction.

- Make sure that your screen shot graphics are captured consistently from monitors of the same resolution. Screen shots captured at different resolutions look different. Full-screen images are more useful than partial images.

Tables, Line Graphs, Pie Charts, and Bar Charts

To show how the same information can be presented in different ways, let's take a look at how we might summarize some data derived from the Bureau of Labor Statistics:

> *The Bureau of Labor Statistics released projections on future job growth by industry and occupation. During the 1994–2004 decade, the percentage of jobs in the service-producing industry grew by 4.4%, while the percentage of jobs in the goods-producing industry declined by 2.6%. From 2004 through 2014, employment growth will continue to be concentrated in the service-providing sector of the economy, with an increase*

of 2.7% projected. Employment in goods-producing industries is expected to decrease from 15% to 13.2% of total employment, a decline of 1.8%.[3]

Although this summary gives some essential information, it would make for a very dry presentation. How about showing your audience what you're talking about? One way to do that is with a table (Figure 6-10).

Figure 6-10 ◆ Labor Statistics in a Table

Employment by Major Industry Sector, 1994, 2004, and Projected 2014			
	1994 Distribution by Percent	2004 Distribution by Percent	2014 Distribution by Percent
Goods-Producing, Excluding Agriculture	17.6	15.0	13.2
Service-Providing	71.4	75.8	78.5
Other	11.0	9.2	8.3
Total	100.0	100.0	100.0

Use tables to:

- Present a large amount of detailed information in a small space
- Facilitate detailed, item-to-item comparisons
- Show numerous facts precisely

To make the use of tables effective:

- Design the table for quick scanning.
- Make the table complete, so that the reader does not need to refer to surrounding text. Give each table a title and column heads.
- Keep the information in the table consistent. For example, include the same number of digits to the right of decimal points for all numbers in a column.

Although a table presents information in a convenient form, it does not enable the reader to see the data. To do that, use line graphs, pie charts, or bar charts (Figures 6-11 through 6-13).

Figure 6-11 ◆ Labor Statistics in a Line Graph

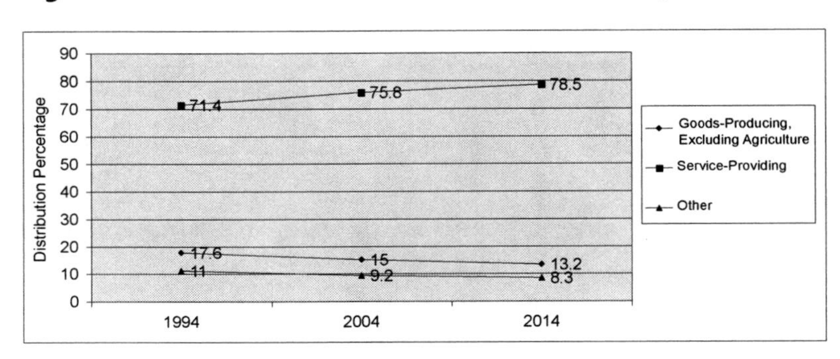

Now you have a better idea of what the change in distribution of jobs looks like. Another way to see this change is through a pie chart. However, a pie chart can show only one year at a time.

Figure 6-12 ◆ Labor Statistics in a Pie Chart

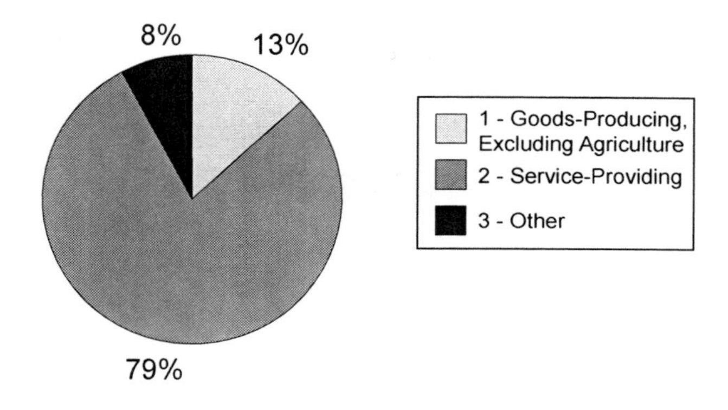

To see all three years depicted side-by-side, you need a bar chart:

Figure 6-13 ◆ Labor Statistics in a Bar Chart

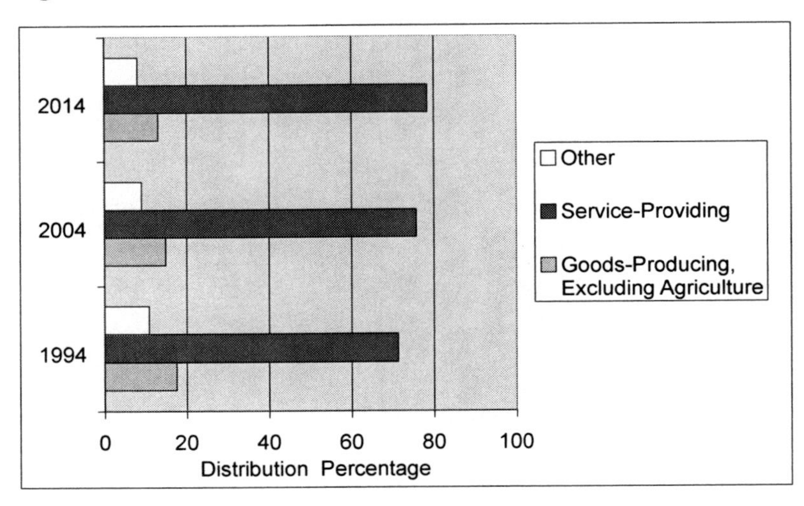

Bar charts can compare various items for a particular time (e.g., Population of the Six Major Regions of the United States, 1900) or show how one item changed over time (e.g., Population of the Middle Atlantic States, 1800–1950). Bar charts can have single or multiple bars. To make bar charts effective:

- Label both the horizontal and vertical axes.
- Make sure all the bars are the same width. The space between the bars should be about one-half the width of the bars.

As you can see, we use specific charts and graphs for specific purposes. It's useful to know when and how to use each graphic most effectively. Use graphs, pie charts, and bar charts to:

- Emphasize trends, relationships, and patterns in the data
- Forecast and predict future trends
- Present large amounts of complex data
- Add credibility
- Induce the reader to read the text

To make their use effective:

- Keep charts simple.
- Focus on the data, displaying it so trends stand out.
- Avoid misleading charts.
- Graduate the vertical and horizontal scales so that they give an accurate visual impression of the data. To prevent distortion, keep the scales in constant ratio with each other.
- Include all titles, notes, and annotations needed to make the chart clear and complete.

- Use similar symbols, textures, or colors for related items of data.
- Use different symbols, textures, or colors to distinguish separate data elements or series.
- Use curves and lines to show trends and to connect data points.
- Include a key and explain symbols when necessary.

In graphics showing information over time, time should flow forward, not backward. For example, in a bar chart showing annual sales revenue from 2006 through 2008, the column for the year 2006 should appear first when going from left to right.

To help your readers understand the information they need, you need to create visually appealing documents. This means using white space, short sections, easy-to-read type, frequent headings, and bulleted and numbered lists, as well as boldface and italic for emphasis.

Graphics also add visual appeal and can aid a reader's comprehension of a document. Some common types of visual aids that you can use to enhance your writing and supplement information include:

- Photographs
- Line drawings
- Cutaway diagrams
- Exploded diagrams
- Maps
- Flow charts
- Schematics
- Screen shots
- Tables
- Line graphs
- Pie charts
- Bar charts

All graphics should be labeled clearly, have a caption, and make sense—even if the reader doesn't read the text.

NOTES

1. John V. Thill and Courtland L. Bovée, *Excellence in Business Communication,* 7th ed. (Upper Saddle River, NJ: Pearson Prentice Hall, 2007), 388.
2. Plain Language Action and Information Network, "Car Safety." Online at http://www.plainlanguage.gov (accessed November 2007).
3. Based on "Bureau of Labor Statistics Releases 2004–14 Employment Projections," Dec. 7, 2005. Online at www.bls.gov/news .release/ecopro.nr0.htm (accessed November 2007).

CHAPTER 7

Editing: The Final Phase

◆ One Step at a Time ◆

Maria's boss, Lee, asked her to edit the manuscript of the new consumer protection handbook. After a few days, Maria handed it back in.

"Great job, Maria," Lee said. "Tell me, how did you manage to do that so quickly and accurately?"

"I did it in several stages," Maria replied. "The first day or so, I looked at the document in its entirety—the big picture. I checked to see that it was well organized, complete, and logical. I made sure the main idea of each section and each paragraph was clear. Next, I copyedited, looking first at the sentences, checking for active voice, subject-verb agreement, and all that. Finally, I checked the spelling, punctuation, and capitalization. When I was done, I had Ryan and Anne each review it. They found some things I had missed."

"Yes, it's always good to have more than one set of eyes look at a document," Lee said.

"And one other important thing," Maria said. "I found that I needed to put it down occasionally and take a break. When I came back, I was able to look at it with fresh eyes."

"Well, keep those eyes fresh," Lee said. "I'll need you to proofread the handbook when it comes back from the printer."

People are often tempted to ignore the final editing phase, but doing so is risky. A thoughtful editorial review is the last line of defense for every document. "It's a shame that editors are so often told, 'Do only a light copyedit; there's not time or money for more,'" says Jane Rea, manager of editorial services for EEI Communications. "You can't skimp on the editing step and still hope to get a readable product."[1]

In his book, *On Writing Well: The Classic Guide to Writing Nonfiction*, William Zinsser gives the following comments about the importance of editing and rewriting:

> *Rewriting is the essence of writing well: It's where the game is won or lost. That idea is hard to accept. We all have an emotional equity in our first draft; we can't believe that it wasn't born perfect. But the odds are close to 100 percent that it wasn't. Most writers don't*

initially say what they want to say, or say it as well as they could. The newly hatched sentence almost always has something wrong with it. It's not clear. It's not logical. It's verbose. It's clunky. It's pretentious. It's boring. It's full of clutter. It's full of clichés. It lacks rhythm. It can be read in several different ways. It doesn't lead out of the previous sentence. It doesn't . . . . The point is that clear writing is the result of a lot of tinkering.[2]

It's important to review your work to make sure that your writing achieves its purpose; your ideas are stated clearly and correctly; and your writing is free of spelling, grammatical, and other mechanical errors. Remember, even professional writers rely on editors to cast a critical eye on their work.

TWO TYPES OF EDITING

When we discuss editing, we are really referring to two different types of critical review: substantive editing and line (or copy) editing. In *substantive* editing, you review the overall development of the writing, looking at how well the ideas are organized and developed and how well they are presented. In *line editing*, you check subject-verb agreement, verb tense, active and passive voice, understandability, precision, and readability, as well as the mechanics of writing, such as spelling and punctuation.

Substantive Editing

During this step, look at the overall picture. Ask yourself, "Did I follow my outline? Did I include the ideas I wanted to include? Did I develop those ideas properly? Did I present them in a logical order? Did I present those ideas in a way that makes them understandable?" In other words, "Did I say what I wanted to say?"

Consider what you've said, and put yourself in the reader's place. Read only what you've put on the page; don't read in what you know but have left unsaid. If possible, have someone who is totally unfamiliar with the subject read what you've written.

The following checklist can help you make sure your writing is doing what you want it to do:

- *Statement of purpose.* Make sure you have included your purpose, and that your ideas and the organization of them help you achieve that purpose.
- *Completeness.* Check your document against your outline to make sure you covered all points.
- *Unity of thought.* If you digressed from your outline, decide whether the departure is justified.
- *Redundancy.* Keep a sharp eye out for places where you have repeated yourself.

- *Audience.* Ask yourself if what you have written is understandable and useful to the people who will read it. You want to say enough to inform them without saying too much.

- *The "bottom line on top."* Check that you put the main idea of your document first. Then check each section to make sure the main idea comes first.

- *Clarity.* Your ideas should be presented clearly and logically, with no ideas hidden or thrown in at the end without being fully developed.

- *White space.* White space between paragraphs makes each paragraph stand out visually. Indents or bullets help show how ideas are subordinate to each other. In this checklist, for example, bullets show that each item is part of the main checklist.

- *Headings and subheadings.* These should help the reader understand your organization.

- *Conclusions.* Make sure they are understandable and that you said enough to support them—but not too much.

- *Transitional words.* These help the reader see the connections between your ideas.

Line Editing (Copyediting)

Once you've looked at the overall picture, it's time to check the smaller details, such as the development of paragraphs and sentences. Now is the time to think about word choice, tone, style, readability, understandability, and precision. As you read over something, think about how it sounds to you.

Line editing also means checking for proper and consistent spelling, punctuation, capitalization, abbreviation, word division, and the like—matters that are sometimes referred to as the *mechanics* of writing. The purpose of line editing is to eliminate any errors or inconsistencies, as well as any awkward features that might distract the reader from what is being said.

The following checklist can help you with line editing:

- *Paragraphs*. Make sure each paragraph covers one main idea and has a topic sentence that introduces that main idea.

- *Sentences*. Each sentence should cover one idea. If a sentence covers more than one idea, decide if it should it be broken into two sentences. Check to see that sentences are varied in structure and in length.

- *Verbs.* Use the active voice, in which the subject of the sentence performs the action, whenever possible.

- *Submerged verbs.* Look for any verbs that have been submerged under helping verbs and turned into nouns (such as, "He made an assessment" instead of "He assessed").

- *Choice of words.* Read your document aloud to see that it is in plain English. Delete or change any of the following:

  – Bureaucratese (e.g., "At this point in time, we estimate that implementing this program will affect . . ." instead of "We now believe this program will affect . . .")

  – Clichés (e.g., "six of one and half a dozen of another")

  – Gobbledygook (e.g., "electronically adjusted, color-coded vehicular-flow control mechanism" instead of "traffic light")

  – Coined words (e.g., "ultra-self-orientationability" instead of "ability to orient itself")

- *Tone.* Make sure your words convey the right amount of friendliness and directness. You don't want to sound overly familiar, arrogant, or unsure.

- *Gender-neutral language.* Avoid using "he" when referring to either male or female. Opt for "flight attendant," not "stewardess"; "police officer" rather than "policeman"; and "humankind" instead of "mankind."

- *Clarity.* Choose simple, direct phrases and familiar words. Look for any stiff, pompous-sounding expressions. Also check that you don't use too many acronyms.

- *Precision.* Make sure you clearly state what you mean. Instead of vague terms ("large book"), use specific words ("559-page novel").

- *Punctuation.* Look for correct use of:

  – Commas

  – Semicolons

  – Colons

  – Periods

PROOFREADING

Your work as a business writer is not truly done until you have seen your manuscript through to the end. You need to *proofread* to make sure that the finished product reflects the care you put into planning, writing, and revising. Although the term "proofreading" originally meant the reading of printers' proofs to detect errors, it now refers to the checking of any final product. You need to double-check for any details that might have slipped by as you pored over your computer screen. It's a good idea to see your manuscript in hard copy to help you spot difficulties.

Sheryl Lindsell-Roberts, author of *Business Writing for Dummies*, says this about proofreading:

> *Proofreading is akin to quality control. In a manufacturing environment, quality control is making sure the merchandise is free from defects so the customer doesn't wind up with a lemon. In the world of writing, it means making sure that the document is free from errors so it reflects well on you, the writer.*[3]

Ask yourself:

- Does the "rule of 10" apply? That is, are all numbers of two or more digits presented as figures, while all one-digit numbers are presented as words? (Check your style manual because this rule can vary.)
- Am I correct in capitalizing Eastern Standard Time?
- Should I insert a comma after the last element of a series—for example: thinking, writing, and editing. (Check your style manual because this rule can vary.)

- When I wrote Tuesday, March 20, did I check to make certain March 20 is a Tuesday?
- Did I double-check the spelling of all names of people, titles, and organizations?
- Did I double-check all numbers?
- Did I write *principle* instead of *principal*, or *it's* instead of *its*?

Frequently Used Proofreader's Marks

Mark	Meaning	Mark	Meaning
⊙	Insert period	^,	Insert comma
:	Insert colon	;	Insert semicolon
?	Insert question mark	!	Insert exclamation point
=/	Insert hyphen	’	Insert apostrophe
“ ”	Insert quotation marks		
1/N	Insert -en dash	1/M	Insert -em dash
[/]	Insert brackets	(/)	Insert parentheses
#	Insert space	⁀‿	Close up
ʃ	Delete	ʃ (with close-up marks)	Delete and close up
stet	Let it stand—used in margin	......	Let it stand—used in text under affected letters
sc	Small caps—used in margin	=	Small caps—used in text under affected letters

Mark	Meaning	Mark	Meaning
caps	All caps—used in margin	≡	All caps—used in text
lc	Lowercase—used in margin	/	Lowercase—used in text on affected letters
¶	Paragraph	No ¶	No paragraph
]	Move right	[	Move left
⌐¬	Move up	⊔	Move down
][	Center horizontally	⊔ ⊓	Center vertically
‖	Align vertically	=	Align horizontally
tr	Transpose—used in margin	∽	Transpose—used in text around affected letters
ital	Italic—used in margin	—	Italic—used in text under affected letters
bf	Boldface—used in margin	~~~	Boldface—used in text under affected letters
/	Used in text to show deletion or substitution	∧	Caret—indicator used to mark position of change

THE EDITING PROCESS

When you're ready to plunge into editing, try to work during the period of the day when you're most alert. For some of us, this is first thing in the morning; for others, it's the afternoon or late at night. Find a quiet place and force yourself to concentrate. *Tackle the job systematically.* Don't try to see too many things at once.

Professional copyeditors have different methods for organizing their work. Some begin with a very slow read, then go back and read quickly the second time through.[4] The following is one way to approach the job:

1. Inventory the materials to make sure you have everything.
    a. If there is more than one page:
        – Does each page have a number?
        – Are the pages in order?
    b. If there is more than one part:
        – Are all the parts (attachments, enclosures, appendices, table of contents, bibliography, exhibits, etc.) included and in order?
        – Is each part labeled correctly and clearly?
        – Are titles and headings typed consistently?
        – Are all footnotes or endnotes included?
2. To begin, focus on groups of words in sentences and paragraphs.
    a. The first time through, read only for *meaning*.
        – Does what is there, on the page, make sense?
        – Has anything been left out?
    b. Next time, check the *mechanics*.

– Are the sentences grammatically correct?

– Is the punctuation correct?

– Are all references and citations accurate?

3. Now try to focus on *individual words.* (Sometimes it helps to read backward, starting with the last word and working back to the first.)

   a. Are there any typos?

   b. Are the words spelled correctly?

   c. Are the words capitalized correctly and consistently?

   d. Are the words abbreviated correctly and consistently?

   e. Are the words divided correctly and consistently?

   f. Are figures and symbols used correctly and consistently?

4. Now look at the document *as a whole.*

   a. Are the parts arranged appropriately and evenly on the page?

   –Are the margins adequate?

   – Does the white space reflect the thought structure?

   – Are the indentations consistent?

   – Is the spacing consistent?

MAKING CHANGES ONLINE

When you're editing online, first make a working copy of each file you plan to edit and put the original files in a safe place. You need to have a backup copy and also might need to consult the unedited original files while you're working on the project. Make sure the working files are labeled differently from the original ones so there will be no confusion. Make a hard copy of each original file.

One useful way to edit online is to track your changes using a program that allows changes to show up in red. Typically, insertions are shown underlined and deletions are shown with strikethrough marks. You can choose to have these red lines show up on the printout or not. If other people edit your work, the highlighted changes make their job much easier. They can focus on your editing and can choose to accept or reject the changes you have made.

HOW CAN A STYLE MANUAL HELP?

A style manual provides guidelines for correctness and consistency regarding the mechanics of language. You're likely to have questions that are not answered in style manuals. Sometimes a good dictionary will help. At other times, you'll have to rely on your preference and judgment. Whatever alternative you choose, use it consistently.

The following are among the most widely used style manuals:

- *The Associated Press Stylebook and Libel Manual* (Reading, MA: Addison-Wesley Publishing Company, 1992). Used by journalists and editors, this stylebook is organized like a dictionary. It contains useful appendices on copyright guidelines, the Freedom of Information Act, photo captions, and proofreaders' marks.

- *The Chicago Manual of Style*, 15th ed. (Chicago: The University of Chicago Press, 2003). Many writers in academia and business consider this the standard style guide. It has many useful sections, including ones on punctuation, quotations, and abbreviations.

- *The United States Government Printing Office Style Manual*, 29th ed. (Washington, D.C.: U.S. Government Printing Office, 2000). This manual is the authority for writers, editors, typists, typesetters, and printers throughout the government. The manual covers matters from capitalization to plant and insect names, and it even has sections on foreign languages. It contains a helpful list of standard proofreading marks. This style manual is also available online at http://www.gpoaccess.gov/stylemanual/browse.html (accessed January 2008).

More specific style manuals are published by the following organizations:

- American Chemical Society
- American Mathematical Society
- American Psychological Association
- Council of Biology Editors
- International Steering Committee of Medical Editors
- Modern Language Association
- United States Geological Survey

Different style manuals might list different rules for printing the same information, depending in part on the needs of those who regularly use the manuals. For a better understanding of how style manuals differ, consider the examples presented in Figure 7-1.

EDITING SOMEONE ELSE'S DOCUMENT

Editing someone else's writing requires objectivity, maturity, and tact. A writer has put time and effort into creating a document and is putting his or her ego on the line when giving it up for editing. Therefore, as an editor, try to be balanced, specific, constructive, and gentle.

Figure 7-1 ◆ Comparing Style Manuals

Style Guide	Abbreviations for state names in conjunction with cities	Capitalization of professional titles	Dates	Foreign words and phrases	Numbers	Decades
AP	Use abbreviations provided ("Birmingham, Ala.")	Capitalize only directly before a name ("Secretary of Defense William Perry")	"Oct. 18, 2001"	Do not italicize; place in quotation marks and explain if unfamiliar	Spell out whole numbers below 10	"the 1990s"
Chicago	Spell out except in tables, lists, reference materials, and addresses	Capitalize only directly before a name ("Secretary of Defense William Perry")	"18 October 2001"	Italicize if likely to be unfamiliar	Spell out whole numbers below 100	"the 1990s"
GPO	Use Postal Service abbreviations ("Birmingham, AL")	In specified instances, capitalize after a name ("William Perry, Secretary of Defense")	"October 18, 2001" (or, in the military, "18 October 2001")	Do not italicize unless specifically requested	Spell out whole numbers below 10	"the 1990's"

First, make sure you know the author's *purpose* for writing the document and the *audience* for whom the document is intended. Determine what level of editing is needed—light, medium, or heavy. This will be determined by the quality of the author's writing, the audience, the production schedule, and the size and importance of the document.

Next, check the materials to make sure they're complete. Read the draft once in its entirety before you make any marks on it. Then ask yourself the questions for substantive editing. When you read the draft through again, consider the points related to line editing.

Only after you have carefully considered your comments should you begin writing—with a pencil, not a pen, so that you can change your comments if necessary. Guidelines for editing someone else's work include:

- Make no change unless you can give a good reason for it.
- Focus on the document and its impact on the intended reader, not on your preferences.
- Use good judgment in responding to what has been written. If a piece of writing is good, return it with a note saying, "Nice work" or "Great job."

- If the document needs substantial editing, take the time to talk to the writer. Suggest some changes you think are necessary and explain why. Provide gentle instruction, not scolding, as needed.

- Remember that your job as an editor is to look at a document objectively—something that is impossible for a writer to do.

FIELD-TESTING YOUR WRITING

It's important to get feedback from people who are likely to use your document. We often write documents that are more suitable for ourselves than for our readers. Make sure that you test what you write. Always have someone else read and comment on what you write.

If you're preparing documents that will be widely circulated, conduct a field test among people who represent your audience. This process will tell you if your audience *wants to read* your work, *can read* it, and *can use* it. The Plain Language Action and Information Network describes three methods of testing: focus groups, protocol testing, and control studies.[5]

Focus Groups

A focus group is run with a small group (usually 8 to 12) people. The moderator prepares a list of questions or a script in advance and might use a one-way mirror for observers or a tape recorder to help ensure an accurate report. The moderator should ask questions that generate discussion and that will not bias the answers.

Although focus groups might give some qualitative—what do people think about it?—information, they are time-consuming and require a skillful moderator.

Protocol Testing

Protocol testing is a qualitative technique that tests the usability of a document. This one-on-one interview with the reader is extremely valuable in determining whether the reader is interpreting your message the way you intended. Here are the steps:

1. Ask the reader to read to a specific cue, usually a dot indicating a stopping point.

2. Each time the reader reaches the cue, ask for an explanation of what that section means.

3. At the end of the document, ask additional questions, such as:

   a. What would you do if you got this document?

   b. Do you think the writer was trying to help you?

4. For longer documents, test the document as a whole, not just individual paragraphs. Note how often the reader has to flip from page to page to find references, for example.

5. Conduct six to nine interviews on each document.

The following is an example of how protocol testing uncovered misunderstanding on the part of readers.

The Veterans Benefits Administration (VBA) tested a letter in which readers appeared to understand every word. However, when asked what they would do if they got this letter, most people said they would call VBA's toll-free number. The letter was about a replacement check sent because the original check was now out-of-date. The letter said, "You will receive the new check shortly." Readers indicated that they would call if they didn't receive the check at the same time as the letter. Changing the sentence to show the approximate date on which they would receive the check eliminated countless phone calls.

In another situation, some readers were confused by the VBA term "service-connected disability." To VBA, it means that a veteran has a disability that can be traced back to his or her time in military service. Protocol tests showed that one veteran thought it meant a disability that had happened at work. Another veteran was injured while in the military, but not while on duty, and did not know whether he had a service-connected disability.

When the readers were asked a general question about understanding the letter, they all said that it was clear. Yet several would have done something different from what VBA wanted because they assumed a different definition of "service-connected." The solution was to explain the phrase so that everyone was working from the same definition.

Control Studies

Control studies allow you to collect quantitative data on how well the public uses the final document you've produced. To conduct a control study, follow these steps:

1. Before you conduct the study, think about what would make your document successful—what kinds of results you want. For example:

   a. Do you want *more calls* regarding a certain program?

   b. Do you want *fewer calls* asking for clarification?

   c. Do you want *more people* to return an application or payment?

   d. Are there certain parts of the application that you would like to be completed *more accurately*?

2. Send a small group of people the new version of your document.

3. Send the same number of people the old version.

4. Ask members of both groups to respond to your document, preferably in writing.

5. Track the responses of both groups.

6. Record responses. (For example, you can record what percentage of your "before document" generates correct responses compared to your "after document.")

It's a good idea to use control studies after your qualitative testing is completed and you believe you have the best possible document. This is because control testing will tell you *if* the new document is a success, but it won't tell you *why* it is or isn't a success.

When to Use Different Tools

Focus groups and control groups are optional, depending on what type of document you are rewriting. However, protocol testing is an essential tool to help you determine where to make changes in your document. Figure 7-2 shows the most effective times to use each method of testing:[6]

Figure 7-2 ◆ Three Methods of Field Testing

Method of Testing	When to Use It	What You Will Get
Protocol Test (qualitative)	• After completing a final draft of your document	• Specific information about what readers think your document means • Information about what readers will do with the document when they receive it • Observations about how they read your document and how well they can follow the format • This should be the basis of any revisions to the document.
Focus Group (qualitative)	• Before rewriting an old, usually lengthy, document • After rewriting to compare the format of different versions of a document	• Information about how readers feel about the old document—what they like and don't like • What information they need that they don't have • This can be a basis for how you rewrite the new document. When focus groups are used to decide on format, the content should already be protocol-tested. The content should be the same for each version.

Method of Testing	When to Use It	What You Will Get
Control Group (quantitative)	• After protocol testing and revising a document	• Data about how many people did what you wanted • A comparison between the old document and the new document • This information can help determine the success of the rewrite.

Joseph Kimble is a strong advocate of document testing:

> *We do need to give more attention to testing major documents, and not just legal documents. Government and businesses send out forms, notices, brochures, and bills by the thousands and hundreds of thousands. Testing a draft costs money. But even some testing is better than none; some kinds of testing are not expensive; and whatever testing is done on mass documents should pay for itself many times over.*[7]

TEST YOURSELF

LINE EDITING A LETTER

Suppose you had written the letter below. What changes would you make before mailing it? Examine the letter for things that look or sound strange. Look out for inconsistencies, omissions, errors, problems with tone and style, submerged verbs, and parts that aren't parallel. Is the letter understandable? Is the phrasing precise? Circle each mistake you notice and rewrite the letter. See the Appendix for a suggested revision of this letter.

Dear Mrs. Phillips;

Thank you for inquiring about changes planned for this year's Youth Leadership Institute (Y.L.I.) program.

Lessons learned from last year

Many participants said that last year's YLI program was the best of its kind. However, the program showed the need to provide 24-hour direction to the program participants. Therefore, Behavioral Sciences has made a suggestion that this year's instructors undergo new screening procedures. This screening would identify whether instructors have the background in psychology needed for providing 24-hr. monitoring of students; crisis counseling abilities; and screening for substance abuse problems.

Last year's student progress evaluation program survey results showed that, despite attempts to compensate for false results caused by students' unwillingness to discuss their concerns, the evaluation program too often did not reflect students' progress accurately.

Changes planned for this year

To address the survey problem, we are developing a new survey system which uses both instructor-led interviews and anonymous questionnaires. Both surveys will be administered frequently. Students will participate in both programs, and instructors will use the anonymous questionnaire results to gauge the overall progress of the students as a body. We hope to optimize this year's survey findings with this new system.

We are also preparing to implement the suggested instructor screening program, with input from Behavioral Sciences and from the Personnel Department.

In view of the fact that we are making these changes, we will send you copies of all pertinent forms and questionnaires when they become available. Please call if you need more info.

Sincerely,

Reviewing your documents is absolutely essential. After spending hours or days preparing a letter or report that you're proud of, you don't want to send it out with even one error because, unfortunately, the error is what your reader will remember.

Reviewing documents includes three steps: substantive editing, line editing, and proofreading. In some cases, you might add an important fourth step: testing.

In *substantive editing,* you look at the big picture—the overall development of your writing. At this stage, you read over your document to make sure it is logical, understandable, complete, well organized, and directed toward the audience.

Next, you *line edit* your document. Now is the time to check the smaller details like development of paragraphs and sentences, usage and spelling of words, and punctuation.

When you have what you believe is your final copy, it's important to double-check for any details that might have slipped by you. Be especially careful to recheck the spelling of all names of people, titles, and organizations; numbers; dates; word usage; capitalization; and punctuation.

A style manual is invaluable during the copyediting and proofreading stages of the writing process. Make sure you're aware of differences among style manuals and that you follow the one your office uses. Use the *U.S. Government Printing Office Style Manual* if you're a federal employee.[8]

When you edit someone else's work, try to be balanced, specific, constructive, and gentle. Your job is to look at a document objectively—something that is impossible for a writer to do.

After you have edited and proofread your document, always have someone else read and comment on what you wrote. If you're preparing documents that will be widely circulated, conduct a field-test among people who represent your audience. Three methods of testing are focus groups, protocol testing, and control studies. Focus groups and protocol testing yield qualitative information, whereas control studies give you quantitative data. All three are useful in specific situations; protocol testing is essential after you have completed the final version of your letter or report.

NOTES

1 Mark R. Miller, "Is It Plain English Yet? Bureaucratese Makes People Read Between the Lines," *The Editorial Eye* 22, no. 3 (March 1999): 1.

2 William Zinsser, *On Writing Well: The Classic Guide to Writing Nonfiction,* 7th ed. (New York: HarperCollins, 2006), 83–84.

3 Sheryl Lindsell-Roberts, *Business Writing for Dummies* (New York: IDG Books Worldwide, 1999), 90.

4 For a thorough explanation of the editorial process, see Amy Einsohn's *The Copyeditor's Handbook,* 2nd ed. (Los Angeles: University of California Press, 2006), 15–19.

5 Plain Language Action and Information Network, "Testing Your Documents." Online at http://www.plainlanguage.gov (accessed November 2007).

6 Ibid.

7 Joseph Kimble, "Answering the Critics of Plain Language," *The Scribes Journal of Legal Writing* (1994–1995). Online at http://www.plainlanguagenetwork.org/kimble/critics.htm (accessed January 2008).

8 Government Printing Office, *The United States Government Printing Office Style Manual,* 29th ed. (Washington, D.C.: U.S. Government Printing Office, 2000). Online at http://www.gpoaccess.gov/stylemanual/browse.html (accessed January 2008).

PART II
Types of Business Writing

CHAPTER 8

Emailing the Right Message

◆ Email: Do the Old Rules Still Apply? ◆

Michelle wanted to request a five-day class in HTML (Hypertext Markup Language) for her administrative assistant, Anne. She decided to email the request to her boss, Chris. To organize her email, she wrote down all the reasons she could think of to support her request. She wanted to highlight Anne's accomplishments and show how the training would benefit both Anne and the division. Michelle also knew that her boss would be concerned about a regional meeting for which Anne had major planning responsibility. The meeting was coming up in January, and the HTML class was scheduled for early December. Michelle wanted to alleviate any concerns that the class would interfere with Anne's responsibilities.

Some of the ideas she jotted down were:

- Anne needs training to help with the agency's website.

- The regional meeting is in January, but planning is 80 percent complete.
- It's possible to get temporary replacement for Anne.
- Anne has a good attendance record.
- She does a lot in the office.
- She's taking on some of Tim's responsibilities for maintaining the website.
- HTML class is December 5–9.
- Anne has handled travel details for participants competently in the past.
- Anne has organized a mailing list.
- She's been an administrative assistant here for five years.
- Evidence that website needs updating: It hasn't been touched in three months.
- December is typically a slow time in our office.

However, the ideas needed to be organized, with the main idea—the purpose for writing and her position—at the beginning. After much thought, Michelle wrote the following email:

TO: Chris Richardson
FROM: Michelle James
DATE: October 22, 2007
SUBJECT: Training Request for Anne Bronson

I'm writing to request permission for Anne Bronson to attend an HTML class December 5–9, 2007. She's asked for the training so she can help update our website.

Need for Training

- Anne will be taking on some of Tim's responsibilities in maintaining the website.
- She can't take on Tim's job until she learns HTML.
- The website has not been updated for three months.
- No one else in the office has the time to take on this job.

Anne's Record

As Anne's supervisor, I have noticed the following about her work:

- Her attendance record is excellent.
- She handles a variety of tasks, from writing reports and website copy to helping with the budget, with competence and careful attention to detail.
- She's been an administrative assistant here for five years and has requested training only once before.

The Annual Regional Meeting: No Problem

Anne is responsible for planning the annual regional meeting in January, but I do not believe the HTML class will interfere with those responsibilities for the following reasons:

- She already has completed 80 percent of what needs to be done.
- She has organized a mailing list.
- She has the time to handle travel details before and after the HTML class.
- December is a slack period in our department, and we can manage with a temporary replacement.

Thank you for considering this request. Please let me know if you have any questions.

An email message is a type of memo, but it has its own unique flavor. Memos formerly were handwritten on paper and distributed within an organization. Although email is now the preferred medium for correspondence within an organization, it's also used to communicate with customers, contractors, and others. An email message can range from an informal one-sentence request or statement to a multipage, confidential analysis of critical policy issues.

When decisions, directives, orders, and other official news must reach many people at several levels within the organization, email provides an efficient vehicle. Even when a message must reach only one person or a small group, sending an email is often wise. An email is a reliable means of:

- Giving specific instructions
- Conveying detailed facts or figures
- Writing a message any time of the day or night
- Replying directly to another person's written or oral request
- Establishing a record to show that certain things have been said or done, or that certain views are held
- Attaching additional information that readers can open if and when they choose

Although email is easy and convenient, it also can be overwhelming. The volume of email doubled between 2005 and 2007: Approximately 6 trillion emails were sent in 2006.[1] Responding to email eats up large chunks of time in the workplace.

Sometimes just trying to decipher what someone is trying to say takes the most time. For this reason, careful planning and review of all electronic communication is a must. You need to pay attention to grammar and spelling even though email is informal. Use complete sentences and appropriate capitalization. Taking care with your email messages shows thoughtfulness and consideration—and gets faster results.

Paying attention to the tone of a message is also important. Many relationships have been damaged by emails sent in the heat of anger. Even in unemotional exchanges, readers often misinterpret tone.

Finally, as an email writer you need to be aware of the legal implications of your messages. There is no such thing as a private email. As recent lawsuits have shown, long-forgotten emails can show up in court.

In this chapter, we will guide you through the tricky waters of email correspondence and share some tips for making these messages more effective.

PLANNING EMAIL

Even when the email you wish to write is short and informal, you should resist the temptation to skip over the planning and outlining stage. As the previous vignette shows, careful planning can turn jumbled thoughts into a well-written, organized message. When you need to send an important email:

1. Take the time to determine your purpose. Think about what effect you hope to have on the reader and what you want the reader to do after reading your message.

2. Assemble any helpful materials (earlier emails, other correspondence, policy statements, regulations, or other documents). Review them before you write.

3. Jot down key facts and note ideas that come to you.

4. Group the facts and ideas that belong together, and establish a logical order of presentation.

Audience

Remember that the reader's first reaction will be to ask, "What is this about? What am I supposed to do?" Consider the reader's role, knowledge of the subject matter, and likely reaction to the topic. Consider the reader's relationship to you. This will help you craft your message and convey the appropriate tone.

ELEMENTS OF EMAIL

Emails usually include the following elements:

- *Heading—which includes the following parts:*
  - *To:*
  - *Copy:* (if copies are being distributed to other people)
  - *From:*
  - *Subject:*
  - *Sent* (date and time)
  - *Importance* (urgent, normal, etc.)
- *Body*

The most important parts of the email are the *subject statement* and the *opening statement*. The subject statement tells readers what the email is about and determines whether they will open it immediately or not. The opening statement conveys the purpose of the email.

Subject Statement

The subject statement is an opportunity to alert the reader immediately to the essence of the email. Many people do not open their emails. They just skim the subject lines to determine which emails are worth their time. Help your readers by creating a subject line that briefly describes the message and helps them to understand whether it is a top priority or can wait. The subject line should:

- Use only the words necessary to convey the subject clearly.
  - "Subject: Good news on ABC Project progress"
- Use words that will get readers' attention.
  - "Subject: Action needed by 1 p.m. today"
- Use names, titles, dates, and other details where helpful.
  - "Subject: Transfer of James L. Jenkins from Planning and Scheduling to Research, Effective March 1, 2008"
- Be broad enough to summarize what is covered but specific enough to highlight the main purpose.
  - "Subject: Office picnic postponed until July 25"
- Use language that readers will understand—technical terms or layperson's terms, as appropriate.

Opening Statement

The first paragraph of the email—preferably the first sentence—should tell why you are writing. State your position or convey the information. Don't make the reader dig to find out what the point is. And don't begin with filler phrases like "The purpose of this email is." Get right to the point:

- "Please review the attached policy and send me your comments by November 17."
- "We should expand this office to provide space for the seven new employees."
- "Would you please bring the pie chart to the next team meeting?"
- "The director approved our proposal for revised accounting procedures."
- "Attached is the information you requested on the public's response to the updated form."

Include all the important information in the opening, including the answers to what, when, where, who, why, and how. Do *not* include unnecessary information.

Well-written email...

- Saves time and avoids misunderstanding
- Contributes to the efficiency of the organization
- Enhances the reputation of the person who wrote it

EMAIL ETIQUETTE (NETIQUETTE)

Although many of the standard rules and niceties apply to emails, a few new ones have cropped up to meet the particular needs of this new type of communication.

Tone and Style

All the writing principles that apply to letters apply equally to email. Adapt your degree of formality to fit the expectations of the intended reader(s) and your purpose. In communicating an official policy, for example, you would want to be far more authoritative, impersonal, and serious than you would in addressing a request to a coworker.

Use the social conventions: Please, thank you, and a friendly close can make the difference between a cold, brusque tone and a warm, courteous one. Use positive words whenever possible, and keep your messages courteous, direct, and brief. Unlike face-to-face communication, written messages cannot be modified by body language and tone of voice. Because of this, they are often misinterpreted. Also, be aware of the recipient's style and try to adapt your style accordingly. For example, if the recipient sends you a long, effusive email, you won't want to send back a curt, three-word reply.

On the other hand, *if you want the recipient of the email to take action, be sure to state what that action is and when you would like it to occur.* Use tact and consideration in framing the request, but be direct and specific about what you want or need.

The Right Recipients and the Right Timing

Communicating to the right person at the right time is just as important when sending an email as it is when sending a letter.

- Send your message to the right person. Make sure your email goes to the person responsible for the activity or function. Do not go over anyone's head. If you don't get results, you should tell the person that you plan to take the matter up with someone in higher authority.
- Hierarchy can be a sticky area, so if you think it's an issue, put the names in the "To" field in the correct order, generally according to rank. You can also go by seniority, familiarity with the issue, or sensitivity to the issue (how much people care about it).
- Send copies to the right people. Send copies of an email to anyone affected by the subject or interested in it. Also send copies to anyone mentioned in the email and to anyone in a direct line of authority between you and the addressee. Do not waste people's time by sending office-wide emails on topics that do not concern most employees.

- When you send an email to a large group, remember that you are sharing private email addresses with the world—addresses that the recipients might prefer not to share. One way to avoid this is to address the email to yourself and put all the recipients on a blind carbon copy (bcc) to preserve their anonymity.

- Prepare your reader for surprising news, especially if it is negative. Call ahead to explain: "You'll be getting an email later today to explain why your budget was cut."

- Send important information to the important people first. Not everyone reads email when it first arrives. Consider sending critical information a day or so ahead to the key people or to those who would be embarrassed if they did not know about it before others.

- Use care in forwarding emails. If you think there is any chance that the sender would not want the message shared, check before forwarding.

Email Nightmare: The Accidental "To"

Most of us have had the embarrassing experience of sending an email to the wrong person, forwarding a message when we thought we were replying, replying to all when we thought we were replying to one person, or continuing an email string that contained embarrassing information.

David Shipley and Will Schwalbe, in their book, *Send: The Essential Guide to Email for Office and Home,* describe an email disaster:

> *In the middle of a computer training session in 2006, the admissions director at the University of California at Berkeley's law school sent the following message to as many as 7,000 applicants: "I'm writing to congratulate you again for being admitted." For the 6,500 of those who hadn't been admitted, this came as a surprise. As did the subsequent retraction that came via email twenty minutes later.*[2]

At least the admissions director realized he had made a mistake and was able to correct his error quickly. Not all of us are so fortunate. It pays to be careful!

Other Guidelines

Other tips helpful in writing emails include:

- Send only one important point per email. If you cover more than one issue in an email, chances are good that at least one point will be forgotten.

- Avoid "screaming." Do not write your email using all capital letters because this is the email equivalent of screaming.

- Don't designate a message urgent unless it *is* urgent. If something is urgent, consider phoning rather than risking that the recipient won't see it in time.

- Inform email recipients when your message does not require a reply. You can simply add "FYI—no reply needed" to the message.

- Keep attachments to a minimum. The larger the attached document, the longer it takes to download and the more memory space it fills on the recipient's computer. Also, many people are wary of attachments because of the possibility of viruses. If you need to send an attachment, it's a good idea to alert the recipient ahead of time.

- Reduce the number of "Thanks!" replies. Such "content-free mail" is not necessary unless (1) the thank-you is really called for, or (2) you need to let the sender know you received the message.

- Be careful when you "reply to all." Make sure that your message is appropriate for every one of the recipients. When you receive a blind carbon copy (bcc), remember that the sender chose not to reveal that you were a recipient. If you use the "reply to all" option, you will disclose to all that you were the recipient of the original email.

- Know when not to write. Highly sensitive or very personal messages are often better communicated in person or off the record. Don't send a message in the heat of anger, and avoid critical, gossipy, or sarcastic messages.

- Use bullets or numbers where appropriate. They help readers pick out your key points. Use numbers when some sequence or priority is required. For example, when giving directions, use numbers to indicate the order in which the steps should be carried out.

- Use emphasis when needed—but use it sparingly. Boldface, italic, underlining, and colored text can draw attention to an important point. Overdoing the emphasis overwhelms the message and implies that you don't trust your reader to find the key points.

SECURITY AND PRIVACY ISSUES

Nothing is private. Even when messages are deleted, they can be accessed on the hard drive by software or online services. Not surprisingly, electronic discovery has become a booming business, expanding from $500 million in 2003 to $2 billion in 2005.[3] Before you click "Send," think about the consequences of someone other than the intended recipient—like your boss—reading the message.

Employers feel they have the right to know if you're using their email system for personal messages, and they sometimes check email. The U.S. government often monitors its messages to protect against email that is being sent for illegal purposes.

Some Land Mines to Avoid

Ever since the use of email began, people have been fired for using it incorrectly. And we've all heard of cases where emails have helped destroy the fortunes of an entire company—Enron, Arthur Andersen, WorldCom, and Merck, for example.

Be especially careful when writing emails that include humor, or emails that require action.

Humor. Humorous email that can be dangerous falls into two categories: office humor (similar to gallows humor) and offensive jokes.

- Office humor. This type of humor surfaces as a way of dealing with tension or difficult problems in the workplace. These emails can be especially damaging because they appear to make light of a serious situation. One example is the following message sent by a frustrated employee at a drug company during legal proceedings involving the diet drug Phen-Phen: "Do I have to look forward to spending my waning years writing checks to fat people worried about a silly lung problem?" The email turned up during court proceedings.[4]

- Offensive jokes. Many people use email to send racist, sexist, pornographic, or otherwise disparaging email. There are many reasons not to send offensive emails, one of which is financial. In April 2006 the U.S. Mint in Denver agreed to pay its female employees almost $9 million to settle sexual harassment claims. Part of the case was based on offensive emails.

Email that requires action. If you receive an email, whether you open it or not, you are presumed to have knowledge of it. Therefore, it is especially important to pay attention to any email that raises problems, especially one that alleges wrongdoing or potentially illegal behavior in your workplace. If you are aware of misbehavior, you must bring that to the attention of management, and you might need to contact counsel.

As a general rule, never send an email if you would not put the same words in a letter or memo or would not want them to be viewed as part of a lawsuit or investigation.

TEST YOURSELF

STATING THE SUBJECT AND PURPOSE

Give each email a more informative subject statement. Then write a one- or two-sentence opening that makes the purpose clear. Suggested answers are available in the Appendix.

SUBJECT: Procedures

Procedures for internal meetings have been a problem in our division for several years. We've discussed what to do about this for the past six months, and at the last divisional meeting, we decided to have Bill come up with a set of procedures. He described them in his March 29 letter. I like what Bill developed and have decided to adopt them.

SUBJECT: Form

I'm sorry it has taken so long for me to get this information to you, but the trainers took forever to send their comments about the updated audiovisual form. They have approved it with slight changes. I have attached the form.

TEST YOURSELF

REWRITING AN EMAIL

Read the email below, and delete all unnecessary and inappropriate information. Then organize the remaining data into a succinct, readable message. Suggested answers are available in the Appendix.

As you know, the division director has been complaining about everyone's writing. He thinks no one can write except him. So it's time to figure out how to set up some training for everyone in business writing skills. You did such a great job setting up the effective meetings course last month that I thought you could organize this one as well. Did I tell you the evaluations for that course were outstanding? Anyway, we have 2 program analysts, 3 budget analysts, 6 engineers, and 4 managers to receive the training. Marsha especially needs the training because the director is really fed up with her. He recommended that we set it up for a three-day course, but two days are fine, too. We need someone to teach it who has experience in the federal service. Do you have any ideas? Thanks so much for helping. I'd recommend that we reserve the seventh floor conference room. However, the director doesn't like that room, so maybe some other one.

Thanks.

Despite electronic mail's ease of use, it requires careful thought, planning, and review. Email is an efficient method for communicating with many people at several levels of an organization. Often it is also the medium of choice for communicating with only one person or a small group, as well as with customers, contractors, and others. An email message can range from an informal one-sentence request or statement to a multipage, confidential analysis of critical policy issues.

The most important parts of an email message are the subject line and the opening statement. The subject line should alert the reader immediately to the essence of the email. It should be broad enough to summarize what is covered but specific enough to highlight the main purpose. The opening statement presents the purpose of the email, its importance to the reader, and the writer's position. Conclusions and recommendations should follow the opening statement.

Following the rules of email etiquette is important. Adapt your tone and style to the purpose of the email. If you want the reader to take action, make sure you state what that action is and when it should be completed. By respecting the rights and the schedules of others, you can send emails when necessary to the right people and avoid sending unnecessary mail.

Before sending an email message, think about the consequences of someone else's reading it. Employers, including the U.S. government, often monitor employee messages.

NOTES

1 Mike Musgrove, "E-Mail Reply to All: 'Leave Me Alone,'" *Washington Post,* May 25, 2007.
2 David Shipley and Will Schwalbe, *Send: The Essential Guide to Email for Office and Home* (New York: Knopf, 2007), 61.
3 Ibid., 200.
4 Jeffrey Steele, *Email: The Manual* (Oak Park, IL: Marion Street Press, 2006), 73–74.

CHAPTER 9

Writing Winning Letters

◆ **When Tact Is Required** ◆

Maria was in a dilemma. She needed to write a letter thanking the man who had spoken at the monthly meeting. Unfortunately, he was a flop. His talk was poorly organized, he had technical problems with his slide show, and he bored his listeners.

"What can I do?" she asked Lee.

"You need to acknowledge the effort and thank him tactfully without exaggerating his talents," said Lee.

Maria worked for a while and then showed Lee the results:

Dear Robert,

We want to thank you for the considerable time and expertise that went into your special presentation at our monthly meeting. It was greatly appreciated.

We can't hear your message about government ethics too often, and you gave our people much to think about. Your energy in the face of technical problems was admirable, especially in the difficult after-lunch time slot.

Please accept our gratitude for your hard work and dedication. Thank you again.

Best regards,
Maria Sanchez

"That's just right for a one-time effort that went wrong," said Lee. "If you plan to ask Robert to speak again, I would follow this letter with some face-to-face advice on how to improve performance."[1]

Every good letter you write will help your organization build good relations with the public and with other organizations. A thank-you letter, for example, is good etiquette. You should send one to anyone who does something for you, even if he or she is paid. In other cases, a letter is often the first contact—and might be the only contact—a person has with your organization.

Improving correspondence allows organizations to serve their clients more efficiently. This chapter shows how to write a clear, well-organized, and persuasive letter.

HOW TO FORMAT A BUSINESS LETTER

Although some communications can be made informally with a phone call or an email, formal situations call for a letter. Letter writing provides you and the recipient with a record of facts, ideas, concerns, and suggestions. Organizing and expressing your ideas in a letter takes thought and time but is well worth the effort. A well-written letter makes a good impression.

For a business letter, you should use good-quality, white paper or letterhead. If possible, limit the letter to one single-spaced page. Include in your letter all the common components in the proper order.

Common Components of a Business Letter

Return Address. Your address or the name and address of the organization that you represent. If you're using letterhead, you don't need this information.

Date. The date follows the return address. There is no consensus on whether you should skip a line between the return address and the date. Some style guides suggest that you do; others do not. You can state the date as *January 6, 2008*, or, if your agency requires, as *6 January 2008*.

Inside Address. Leave two blank lines after the date. Then type the name, organization, and address of the person to whom you are writing. The inside address should include the recipient's title (e.g., Mrs., Ms., Mr., Dr.). Also, make sure you copy the name of the organization exactly as the organization writes it. If you don't know the name of the recipient, or if you're not sure whether the recipient is a man or a woman, make a phone call and try to find out. If you can't, address the salutation to a department or position name—"Dear Personnel Department" or "Dear Chairperson," for example.

Salutation. For the salutation, type "Dear," follow with the person's title and name, and end with a colon. If you want to convey a friendly, familiar tone, use a comma instead.

Subject or Reference Line. Type "Re:" and follow the colon with the reference or main purpose of your letter. Place the subject line two lines below the salutation. It's part of the body of the letter, not the heading.

Body. The actual message is contained in the paragraphs between the salutation and the complimentary close—the body of the letter. These paragraphs should be single-spaced, with a blank line left between paragraphs. You can indent the first line of each paragraph (indented style) or leave all lines flush left (block style).

Complimentary Closing. Leave two spaces after your last body paragraph, and then use a closing, such as "Sincerely yours," "Cordially," or "Respectfully." Note that only the first word of the complimentary close is capitalized. Follow the closing with a comma.

Signature. Write your signature below the closing. Use both your first and last names unless you've established a personal relationship with the person to whom you're writing.

Name and Professional Title. Four lines after the closing, type your full name. Put your professional title below your name.

End Notations. Under the signature block, abbreviations with important functions are often used.

– Initials. If someone other than the writer types the letter, put the writer's initials, then a slash, and then the typist's initials: "JD/MTS" or "jd/mts."

– Copies. If you send a copy of a letter to someone other than the person addressed, use "cc:" and the person's name. For multiple persons, use "cc:" only once and list the persons vertically in alphabetical order or by rank.

– Enclosures. Use "Enc." if you enclose something in the letter and want to make sure the recipient sees it. For more than one enclosure, use Enc. and the number of enclosures—"Enc. 2," for example.

LETTER STYLES

The two main styles of business letters are block and indented. The following are examples of each.

The Block Form

Your organization (if needed)
Your return street address
Your city, two-letter state abbreviation, and ZIP Code
Date

First and last names of the person to whom you are writing with appropriate title
Name of organization
Street address
City, two-letter state abbreviation, and ZIP Code

Salutation: (Dear Mr./Ms. Person):

Reference line:

The body paragraphs in a business letter should be single-spaced. However, you should double-space between paragraphs when your letter contains more than one paragraph.

When you use the block form, use a 1-inch margin all around. Make sure that you format the paragraphs so that all information is flush left.

Complimentary closing,

(Signature)

Your typed name and title

The Indented Form

Your organization (if needed)
Your return street address
City, two-letter state abbreviation, ZIP Code
Date

First and last names of the person to whom you are writing with appropriate title
Name of organization
Street address
City, two-letter state abbreviation, and ZIP Code

Salutation: (Dear Mr./Ms. Person):

Reference line:

The body paragraphs in a business letter should be single-spaced. However, you should double-space between paragraphs when your letter contains more than one paragraph. Use a 1-inch margin all around.

Indent the first line of each paragraph one-half inch. Note that your address and the date are centered, while the inside address is flush left. Instead of placing the closing and signature lines flush left, type them in the center, even with the address and date above.

Complimentary closing,
(Signature)
Your typed name and title

BASIC STEPS IN WRITING BUSINESS LETTERS

Following a few basic rules will help you to write better business letters:

- Rule 1. *Determine your purpose.* Are you writing to inform or to persuade? Plan before you write.
- Rule 2. *Identify your audience.* Think about the role, attitude, and background information the reader has.
- Rule 3. *Know your subject.* Review correspondence and other information, and talk to anyone who can provide additional information.
- Rule 4. *Put the message in sequence.* Present your ideas in a logical order. Organize your letter according to your purpose. Good organization saves time—for you and your reader. You can write the letter right the first time, and your reader can get the message at first reading.
- Rule 5. *Immediately identify the subject and give your position.* Explain why you are writing in the first paragraph—or in the first sentence if you can. Let your readers know why they should read the letter and what your position is.

- Rule 6. *Create a paragraph for each step in the process.* Keep paragraphs short. Use headings and subparagraphs to make the structure clear.

- Rule 7. *Include only what your reader must know to understand, agree, or act.* Use enough detail to make things clear, but not so much that the reader loses the big picture.

- Rule 8. *End by pointing the way ahead.* Tell the reader what is to happen next.

Begin the Letter

Get right to the point! Many business writers ignore this principle. Some mumble for a while before they get to the main idea:

- "The object of this letter is to ask your cooperation regarding one of your former employees who has now applied for employment with this agency. We would much appreciate it if ...."

Others start off with a meaningless acknowledgment:

- "We received the form you sent us by return mail earlier this month."

Instead, tell the reader immediately why you are writing:

- "This letter is to inform you that Section 6 of the St. George's Hundred Project has not been accepted by the James City Service Authority for the following reasons:"
- "The Master Plan for St. George's Hundred Project was approved by the Planning Commission on February 5, 2000."

Give a Point of Reference

If you're answering a message from your reader, it's a good idea to give the reader a point of reference. But don't bore the reader with irrelevant detail. Instead, use a brief reference line:

- "Re: Your letter of April 30, 2007"
- "Re: Application Form XXX-XX-XX"

Or, refer to the topic of the reader's previous message in the first sentence of your letter.

- "I am pleased to inform you that your June 15, 2007, application has been approved by our evaluation branch."

There is one exception to the principle of stating your purpose in the first paragraph. When your message is likely to be distasteful or disappointing to the reader (that is, when you have to say "no"), you might want to let the facts speak first and then state the purpose. In other words, you might want to put the bad news at or near the end of the message. In this way, you prepare the reader for the worst—or present your evidence first to help prevent any further argument.

The following is a sample of a "no" letter:

> September 20, 2001
>
> Thank you for the article you submitted for publication in the *Oakville Journal.*
>
> We have been blessed with an outpouring of articles since September 11, many of them with wonderful ideas. We only wish that we could publish them all, but we simply do not have the space to do so.
>
> Although we are unable to accept your article for publication, we hope that you will submit another one ot us in the future on a different topic. If you have any questions, please feel free to contact the editorial staff.

Organize the Body of the Letter

In the body of your letter, you give information to support the position you stated in the first paragraph. For example, if you're trying to convince upper management to adopt a revised telework policy (a letter of persuasion), you would give your reasons and the data that support your reasons in the body of your letter.

The Inverted Pyramid

Chapter 2 suggested some methods for organizing documents. The method of organization you choose will depend on the type of information you're presenting. For most letters, however, the inverted pyramid is an ideal structure (see Figure 9-1). In this structure, the most important idea goes first (the broad top of the inverted pyramid), the second most important idea follows, and so on.

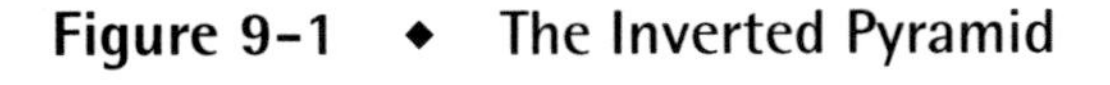

Figure 9-1 ◆ The Inverted Pyramid

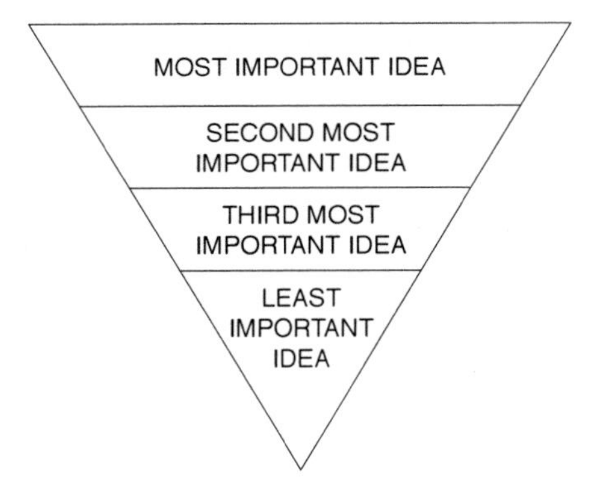

The inverted pyramid is the model for news writing. Journalism students learn early on that it is best to organize newspaper articles with the most important information first. There are two reasons for this: newspaper readers and newspaper editors.

Newspaper readers often do not read more than the headline and the first few paragraphs. Putting the who, what, where, when, why, and how up front gives busy readers the basic information they want and allows them to decide whether to read further for more details.

Newspaper editors know that readers don't read every word and that information should be arranged in an inverted pyramid. They often cut articles from the bottom up to fit the available space.

Writing to More Than One Audience

You may be talking to exporters and importers, coal miners and surface owners, or airlines and passengers. Break your letter down into essential elements and determine which elements apply to each part of your audience. Then group the elements according to who is affected. You might create a table for this purpose to help the reader find pertinent information.

The Plain Language Action and Information Network gives an example of how to treat more than one audience by addressing each subpart separately, instead of grouping them all together:[2]

> Title 40—Protection of Environment
>
> Chapter I—Environmental Protection Agency
>
> Part 745—Lead-Based Paint Poisoning Prevention In Certain Residential Structures
>
> * * *
>
> Subpart E—Residential Property Renovation
>
> *(Firms renovating structures)*
>
> * * *
>
> Subpart F—Disclosure Of Known Lead-Based Paint And/Or Lead-Based Paint Hazards Upon Sale Or Lease Of Residential Property
>
> *(Sellers/Leasors)*
>
> * * *
>
> Subpart L—Lead-Based Paint Activities
>
> *(Training programs)*
>
> * * *
>
> Subpart Q—State And Indian Tribal Programs
>
> *(States and Tribes)*
>
> * * *

HOW TO END THE LETTER

Give your business letter an "action ending" whenever possible. The ending of your letter answers the question,

"What next?" You tell what you want your readers to do, what you plan to do, and the schedule for that action.

What Readers Should Do

- "Please let me know by July 10 what you decide to do about filling the position. You can reach me during business hours at the phone number below."
- "I look forward to seeing you at our meeting on September 18. Please call me if you need directions or have any other questions."

What You Intend to Do

"I'll get in touch with you next week."

"If you approve this plan, I will call and get bids from the three companies next week."

Other

Occasionally, you might just end the letter by saying:

- "Thank you for bringing this matter to our attention."
- "Thank you for taking the time to consider my ideas."

- "We regret any inconvenience that we might have caused you."

Never present new ideas or raise new issues in ending a letter. If you hint about topics that you haven't discussed, you will only bewilder and frustrate your reader.

SPECIFIC TYPES OF BUSINESS LETTERS

Common types of business letters include letters of persuasion, legal writing, letters of recommendation, and letters accompanying reports. Each of these letters has a specific objective, a particular form of organization, and a distinct tone.

Letters of Persuasion

On occasion, you might need to write a letter asking the recipient(s) to do something—recycle motor oil, use child safety seats, or send in a form, for example. When you need to write a letter of persuasion, it's a good idea to follow the model used for sales letters:

- *Open* with a device to get the reader's attention:
  - Involve the reader in some way
  - Offer a benefit
  - Make a startling statement or present a surprising statistic

  - Ask a rhetorical question

- Use the *body* of the letter to:
  - Show how the proposal will benefit the reader
  - Explain exactly what you have in mind
  - Emphasize the main features of the proposal

- Near the *end* of the letter:
  - Ask the reader for a specific action
  - Remind the reader of the benefit

- Create a sense of urgency.

- Make your writing positive and energetic *throughout*.

- Make your letter visually pleasing and professional.

- Make it easy for your readers to respond to the letter. Include information on how to contact you or when you'll contact them (and make sure you do).

- Consider adding a postscript (P.S.). The postscript is the most-read part of a sales letter. Try a handwritten note to personalize the letter.

In Chapter 12 we discuss how to compose a budget justification statement, which is similar to a letter of persuasion.

IRAC (Issue, Rule, Application, Conclusion) System of Legal Writing

Regardless of whether you must write legal letters, it's useful to know how to use the IRAC system of writing. This technique is used when the need to apply a rule or regulation to a specific situation arises. The IRAC system is a useful format for organizing your thoughts when you need to set forth an argument in a step-by-step process. The end product is a logical, coherent, cause-and-effect discussion.

The following example shows how to use the IRAC system.[3]

- *Issue.* Did John Kane violate agency ethics regulations when he accepted free tuition to a professional conference on the latest trends in government accounting?

- *Rule.* Ethics Rule 2.1 prohibits acceptance of any gratuity by a government employee from an organization seeking to do business with the government.

- *Application.* John Kane's action involved acceptance of a gratuity. The course tuition had a dollar value of $325, and the conference sponsor was an organization seeking to do business with his agency.

- *Conclusion.* John Kane violated ethics regulations and is therefore subject to discipline.

Letters of Recommendation

Nearly everyone is asked to write a letter of recommendation at one time or another. The following are some guidelines:

1. Review a copy of the candidate's personal statement or application essays so that your letter of recommendation can dovetail with—not conflict with or duplicate—the rest of the application.

2. Ask the applicant for additional information, such as a resume.

3. Give the candidate's full name and the position or other objective the candidate is seeking.

4. Describe your qualifications for comparing the candidate to other candidates:

    - "I have personally supervised 10 interns every summer for the past 5 years in addition to working with more than 200 college graduates in my capacity as training officer for the Recreation Department."

5. Discuss how you know the candidate:

    - "I have been Ms. Martin's direct supervisor for the past two years."

6. Choose two or three qualities that you observed in the candidate:

    - "Dr. Wood's dedication to his work set a fine example for the entire team. His mentoring and encouragement of new employees will continue to benefit the agency for some time to come."

7. In discussing these qualities, support your statements with specific instances in which the person demonstrated those attributes. Be as concrete and detailed as possible.

    - "Donald's thorough knowledge of databases saved us time and money."

8. Compare the candidate's potential with that of peers, if available:

    - "Ms. Jones consistently rated in the top 10 percent of her class."

9. Discuss the candidate's potential in his or her chosen field

    - "Because of his intelligence, resourcefulness, and strong interpersonal skills, I enthusiastically recommend Mr. Morales for any intermediate or senior marketing position."

Letters Accompanying Reports

When you attach a report, write a brief letter letting the reader know what the report is about. The following is an example:

> *Dear Federal Employee,*
>
> *During the past fiscal year, we at OPM reached out to the human resources (HR) community to assess how well we are meeting the needs of our customers. We developed two customer satisfaction surveys: one for HR directors and one for HR specialists. We received responses from 43 HR directors and 1,340 HR specialists in the field and headquarters.*
>
> *Each survey primarily asked our customers to rate our policy leadership, our efforts to involve agencies in policy development, how well we provide technical assistance, and how effectively we are sharing technical information. On the next two pages you will find some of the key findings from the survey data, which reflect evaluations of all of our program areas. Although we are pleased that many of the responses indicated high levels of satisfaction, there are areas where we need to improve. This is the first time we have received a comprehensive "report card" from our customers, and we are excited at the prospect of working with the HR community to make our service even better.*
>
> *Janice Lachance*
> *Director, Office of Personnel Management*

FORMATTING YOUR LETTERS TO INCREASE EFFECTIVENESS

You can use many techniques to format your letters in a way that gets your message across effectively. Some specific formats include indented lists using bullets or numbers, headings, question-and-answer formats, and if-then tables.

Using Indented Lists

Listing your points with numbers or bullets can make a series of items clearer and more convincing. However, the items in a list should be related to one another in a clear way and should be well organized. The following are guidelines for lists:

- *Lists must contain items of the same classification.* To create an effective list, you must sort your information into appropriate categories. For example, you should not mix causes and effects.

- *Lists must have parallel construction.* Items in a list must have the same grammatical construction and begin with the same part of speech. For example, if the first point in the list is a complete sentence, every other point in the list must be a complete sentence. If the first point begins with an infinitive (such as "to begin"), every other point in the list must begin with an infinitive.

The following before and after examples show the usefulness of indented lists, as well as the importance of conciseness. This is a no-smoking regulation from the Federal Motor Carrier Safety Administration:[4]

Before

Each carrier shall take such action as is necessary to ensure that smoking by passengers, drivers, and other employees is not permitted in violation of this section. This shall include making appropriate announcements to passengers, the posting of the international no-smoking symbol, and the posting of signs in all vehicles transporting passengers in letters in sharp color contrast to the background, and of such size, shape, and color as to be readily legible. Such signs and symbols shall be kept and maintained in such a manner as to remain legible and shall indicate that smoking is prohibited by Federal regulation.

After

To ensure that passengers, drivers, and other employees don't violate the smoking ban in this section, each carrier must:

- Announce to passengers that smoking is prohibited; and
- Post and maintain international no smoking symbols and legible no smoking signs in all vehicles that transport passengers.

Using Headings

Headings are subjects or titles for the sections of your document. They are signposts that help your reader follow what you're saying.

What Headings Do

Headings should do more than simply indicate the part of the document in which the readers have found themselves (e.g., Introduction, Chapter 1). Headings should also summarize the main points of those sections, much like a newspaper headline (e.g., Introduction: Average Credit Card Debt at Record High as Savings Rates Fall).

Like your paragraphs, your headings notify readers when you move from one topic to another. Headings also break up what can be the unremitting grayness of the text. Make sure that you include a heading or subheading every few pages. Spence recommends that you use two headings per single-spaced page to break the text of documents that are more than one page.[5]

The following are some tips for writing headings:

1. *Brainstorm* for words, phrases, or questions that best pinpoint your topic. Don't hesitate to rewrite your headings a few times. It's worth the effort. To compose an effective heading, ask yourself, "What am I going to say in this section?"

2. *Make headings specific and accurate.* Try to give more information, rather than less. Readers should be able to get the gist of a document and see your logic at a glance by reading the headings in the table of contents.

3. *Use an action verb* whenever you can. "Hire a Staff Accountant" is better than "Staff Accountant."

4. Be sure to *use the active voice.* Use "Recommendations Improve Employee Training" rather than "Employee Training Improved by Recommendations."

5. *Be sure the headings flow* in a logical sequence and cover all of your main points.

6. Like items in a list, *headings should be parallel.* For example, all of the following headings begin with *–ing*:

   - Opening a Document File
   - Creating a Data Base
   - Revising Data Base Entries
   - Exporting Files to Other Programs
   - Consulting the System Dictionary
   - Checking for Errors and Inconsistencies

Make the Headings Long Enough to Be Descriptive

Instead of:	**Write:**
Overview	How Staff Attorneys Can Benefit From Using the LAWNET Data Base
Accounting Report	2007 Versus 2006 Annual Revenues
Business Plan	A Proposed Schedule for Opening Three New Branch Offices

How Headings Can Help

Headings can help make a letter clearer, especially if the letter is long or complex. The following are two versions of the same letter, the first *without* headings and the second *with* headings.[6]

Letter Written in Traditional Format

VETERANS BENEFITS ADMINISTRATION
Change in Enrollment Status
Addressee:
Street:
City:
State/ZIP Code:

Dear Addressee:

This letter regards the change in your enrollment status during the term that began September 1, 1996. If the change was due to unavoidable events beyond your control, please notify us as soon as possible. Otherwise, you may be held responsible for an overpayment, or an additional overpayment of benefits.

When giving the reasons for your enrollment change, be as specific as possible. Explain what interfered with your enrollment, give important dates (such as the beginning and ending dates of an illness), and state how your enrollment was affected. In most cases, we will be able to accept your reason only if you submit supporting evidence (such as a doctor's certification to verify an illness, a statement from your employer to confirm a required change in work schedule, etc.).

If you show sufficient grounds for making this enrollment change, any necessary reduction or termination of your award will be effective no earlier than the date your enrollment status actually changed. If your evidence does not establish that the change was caused by unanticipated circumstances beyond your control, or if you do not respond within 30 days, your award must be reduced to the rate of $0 effective the first day of the term in which the change took place.

You withdrew from one or more courses on November 5, 1996. Currently, your award has been reduced effective December 1, 1996. You will receive a computer-generated letter with more details, including the amount of overpayment, if any. If you do not provide acceptable reasons for this course change, your check due on or about January 1 may be reduced or not issued at all due to an additional overpayment.

You will be notified when the decision is made on your case.

Letter Written with Headings

VETERANS BENEFITS ADMINISTRATION
Change in Enrollment Status
Addressee:
Street:
City:
State/ZIP Code:

Dear Addressee:

This letter is about the change in your enrollment during the period that began on September 1, 1996. Because of this change, we might have paid you more than you were due.

What Our Records Show
You reduced your credit hours from 12 hours to 6 hours on November 5, 1996.

What We Did
We reduced your payments on December 1, 1996, to $202.00 per month. You will receive another letter about this change. The letter will show whether you have a debt.

What We Need
Please send us a statement explaining why you reduced the number of your credit hours. In most cases, we require evidence to support your statement. If you do not have supporting evidence, please tell us why. (See the enclosure, *Changes in Your Enrollment.*)

When We Need It
Send us your statement with any supporting evidence within 30 days.

What We Will Do
If we accept your statement, we will not reduce your payments from the beginning date of the term. If a debt has already been created, it must be repaid, but the debt will not be increased.

If we do not accept your statement with supporting evidence, we will reduce your payments on September 1, 1996, the beginning date of the term. This will create a debt that you must repay.

If you do not respond within 30 days, we will reduce your payments on September 1, 1996, the beginning date of the term. This will create a debt that you must repay. Although we will take this action, we will consider information received from you within one year from the date of this letter. (We may extend this time limit if you show a good reason why you could not meet it.)

Your Rights
Basic rights are available to you before we make a final decision on your claim. (See the enclosure, *Basic Rights*.)

Sincerely,

Enclosures:
VA Form 21-4138
Changes in Your Enrollment
Basic Rights
If You Need Help

Using a Question-and-Answer Format

The reader comes to your letter with questions that he or she needs answered. It's more efficient to anticipate the reader's questions and pose them as he or she would. By doing this, you make it easier for the reader to find information.

Since the question-and-answer format assumes that the reader is the one asking the questions, use "I" in questions to refer to the reader. In responses, your organization (represented by "we") addresses the reader.

Figure 9-2 shows the original version of a regulation with short headings that did not help the reader with specific information. On the right are rewritten headings, formatted to fit the reader's needs.

Figure 9-2 ◆ Sample Question-and-Answer Format

Special Grants for Economic Development and Core Management Grants to Small Tribes	Economic Development and Core Management Grants to Small Tribes
§ 254.11 Indian Rights	§ 254.11 How do the procedures in this part affect Indian rights?
§254.12 Applications	§ 254.12 How do I apply for a grant under this part?
§ 254.13 Multi-tribal Grants	§ 254.13 Can a multi-tribal organization submit a single grant request?
§ 254.14 Administrative Requirements	§ 254.14 When must I submit my application?
§ 254.15 Appeals	§ 254.15 What special information is required for an appeal by a multi-tribal organization?

Using "If-Then" Tables

If material is particularly complex and many conditional situations are involved, put an if-then table in your letter. Tables help your reader see relationships in a way that dense text never can. No one would dispute that the rewritten regulation below is far clearer than the dense text it replaces.

Before

§ 163.25 Forest management deductions.

(a) Pursuant to the provisions of 25 U.S.C. 413 and 25 U.S.C. 3105, a forest management deduction shall be withheld from the gross proceeds of sales of Indian forest land as described in this section.

(b) Gross proceeds shall mean the value in money or money's worth of consideration furnished by the purchaser of forest products purchased under a contract, permit, or other document for the sale of forest products.

(c) Forest management deductions shall not be withheld where the total consideration furnished under a document for the sale of forest products is less than $5,001.

(d) Except as provided in § 163.25 (e) of this part, the amount of the forest deduction shall not exceed the lesser amount of ten percent (10%) of the gross proceeds or, the actual percentage in effect on November 28, 1990.

(e) The Secretary may increase the forest management deduction percentage for Indian forest land upon receipt of a written request from a tribe supported by a written resolution executed by the authorized tribal representatives. At the request of the authorized tribal representatives and at the discretion of the Secretary the forest management deduction percentage may be decreased to not less than one percent (1%) or the requirement for collection may be waived.[7]

After

§ 163.25 What forest management deductions will BIA withhold?

We will withhold a forest management deduction if the contract for the sale of forest products has a value of over $5,000. The deduction will be a percentage of the gross proceeds (i.e., the price we get from the buyer). We will determine the amount of the deduction in accordance with the following table.

If . . .	Then . . .
A tribe requests an increase in the deduction through a tribal resolution and written request to us . . .	The percentage of the deduction is equal to the percentage requested by the tribe
An authorized tribal representative requests and we approve a decrease in the deduction . . .	The percentage of the deduction is equal to the percentage requested, with a 1 percent minimum.
An authorized tribal representative requests, and we approve, a waiver of the deduction . . .	The percentage of the deduction is waived.
None of the above conditions apply . . .	The percentage of the deduction is the same as that in effect on November 28, 1990, or 10 percent, whichever is less.

TEST YOURSELF

REWRITING A LETTER

Rewrite the following letter[8] using any of the techniques discussed in this chapter—indented lists, headings, question-and-answer formats, and if-then tables—that seem appropriate. A suggested revision is available in the Appendix.

To: All School Bus Drivers

Re: Limiting Bus Idling

The State School Transportation Association has teamed up with the State Environmental Agency and the Greentown School District to protect schoolchildren and each of you from excessive exposure to diesel exhaust emissions. As part of this effort, we support and encourage you to follow their guidelines restricting engine idling time whenever practical, effective immediately.

To the extent possible, eliminate idling by taking a few simple steps. While waiting for passengers to board at place of origin, shut off all engines. When arriving at your location, shut off all buses as soon as it is practical.

Also, we ask that you follow guidelines for maximum engine idling, which are consistent with existing state regulations. Do not idle more than 3 minutes when the temperature is above 32° F. When the temperature is between −10° and 32° F, limit idling to 10 minutes. If the temperature is below −10° F, there is no limit.

Please help us do our part to reduce air pollution and protect children's (and your own) health. Minimizing vehicle idling will also save money by reducing fuel consumption and engine wear.

Thank you for your support and cooperation with this effort.

Greentown School Bus Drivers Doing Their Share for Clean Air!

Sincerely yours,

Fleet Manager

Well-written letters are a reflection on both you and your organization. Letters should be clearly organized and directed to the specific audience(s) to which they are addressed. Give the main point of the letter first, unless you are conveying bad news.

Use headings to share your structure with the reader and serve as signposts. Use specific, accurate headings with active verbs. Make sure the headings are parallel and that they flow logically.

Using a question-and-answer format in your letter helps the reader find the information needed. Likewise, if-then tables guide the reader through a document, especially a complex one with many conditional situations.

NOTES

1 Adapted from Anne Basye, *Business Letters Ready to Go!* (Lincolnwood, IL: NTC Business Books, 1998), 110. Used with permission.
2 Plain Language Action and Information Network, "Address Separate Audiences Separately." Online at http://www.plainlanguage.gov (accessed January 9, 2008).
3 Donald G. Rider, *Effective Writing for Feds* (Huntsville, AL: FPMI Communications, 1992).
4 Plain Language Action and Information Network, "No Smoking: Federal Motor Carrier Safety Administration." Online at http://www.plainlanguage.gov (accessed January 2008).
5 Padraic Spence, *Business Writing: The Good, the Bad, and the Ugly* (Stockbridge, MA: The Water Street Press, 1996), 112.
6 Plain Language Action and Information Network, "Government Examples of Plain Language Writing." Online at http://www.plainlanguage.gov (accessed November 2007).
7 Plain Language Action and Information Network, "Use Tables to Make Complex Material Easier to Understand." Online at http://www.plainlanguage.gov (accessed January 8, 2008).

8 Adapted from U.S. Environmental Protection Agency and the Maine Department of Environmental Protection, "Maine Idling Letter." Online at http://www.epa.gov/ne/eco/diesel/assets/pdfs/maine_idling_letter.pdf (accessed November 2007).

CHAPTER 10

Creating Rousing Reports

◆ **Conveying Information Professionally** ◆

Maria and Tom had a chance to talk during lunch. The conversation led to their writing projects.

"What advice can you give me about writing reports?" asked Tom. "I have a report to write on last month's site visits."

"Well, remember, although reports are not as conversational as letters," Maria said, "you want your report to convey a friendly, but professional tone.

"Also, reports need to be definite and specific. Don't qualify your statements with phrases like 'I think maybe' or 'in most cases' unless you feel you have to. And whenever you can, back up your statements with evidence or examples. For example, here's a paragraph from a report I just received from our Research Office:

We have concluded that the monthly visit approach works best. In the four months since we have been using it, we have

> *been able to obtain twice as much useful information in less than half the time. While we used to spend an average of 24 hours a month, we now spend 10 or 11. The information we obtain is more useful because ....*
>
> "You get the gist."
>
> "I see what you mean," said Tom. "That's very clear and precise. Thanks so much."

A report is an impartial, objective, planned presentation of facts. It should be logical, accurate, reliable, and easy to read.

Every year hundreds of thousands of government employees get involved in at least some phase of the study/report process. Some volunteer; others are summoned to the task. A number of tasks in government require reports. They include:

- Preparation of legislation
- Development of policies and procedures
- Staffing
- Program analysis
- Employee evaluation
- Job description

- Budget preparation
- Office design
- Workflow analysis
- Office organization
- Strategic planning
- Annual planning
- Public relations

Reports can be *informal* or *formal,* depending on their length, complexity, and intended audience. In this chapter, we discuss the organization of both informal and formal reports, as well as the formats for a number of different kinds of reports.

BASIC PARTS OF AN INFORMAL OR BRIEF REPORT

An informal report might be communicated in the form of an email or a written memo. The elements of a good report fall into three categories:

- Introduction
- Body
- Conclusion

Tips for the Introduction

The opening statement, or introduction, should set the stage for what will follow. It should let the reader know what to expect and make the reader want to read on.

Here are three basic approaches to writing openings:

- Tell the reader what topics you will discuss in the report and their significance to the reader (big picture).
- Let the reader know what you think about, or how you will approach, the topics you will discuss (position statement).
- State conclusions and recommendations, which you will then explain and discuss in the rest of the report.

You may also use a combination of these approaches. In any case, the opening should be no longer and no more complicated than necessary. And it should be written with your reader's needs and interests in mind.

Tips for the Body

The main purpose of the body of the report is to describe or analyze. The body of the letter presents your data and background information.

- In *describing,* you attempt to tell a story. Examples are:
  - Relating what has happened over the past month
  - Detailing what you have observed about a particular problem situation
  - Spelling out the steps involved in performing a task
- In *analyzing,* you look more closely and make some sense of things. For example:
  - Spelling out trends that you have noticed over the past month
  - Providing an explanation of why a problem situation has developed
  - Explaining why particular steps are taken in getting a job done

Whether you use the description approach or the analysis approach, you should decide on a logical way to organize your report. Common ways of organizing include:

- Inverted pyramid
- Order of familiarity

- Order of location (spatial or geographic order)
- Alphabetical order
- Chronological order
- Category order
- Inductive order
- List
- Order for comparison
- Deductive order
- Statement of reasons method
- Comparative advantages method
- Problem-solution method
- Most acceptable to least acceptable
- Comparison/contrast

Tips for the Conclusion

The closing of a report is crucial. It is where you convey the thoughts and impressions you want to leave with your reader.

Three basic approaches—which can also be used in combination—include:

- Give the reader a concise, "in a nutshell" summary of what you have said
- Make final recommendations
- Spell out actions you plan to take

Like the opening, the closing should be to the point. Say what you have to say firmly and briefly. Also like the opening, the closing should be aimed directly at your reader. Ask yourself: What wrap-up would be most helpful, most understandable, and most convincing to my reader?

FORMAL REPORTS

Formal reports are generally longer than informal reports. They often provide comprehensive accounts of major technical projects such as:

- Reports on new developments in a field
- Recommendations on whether to launch a new product or service
- Accounts of activities within the organization

The length and complexity of the report depend upon the length and complexity of the project. Elements of formal reports include:

- Title page
- Any letters relevant to the report
- Executive summary (sometimes called abstract)
- Table of contents
- List of figures (if appropriate)
- List of tables
- List of abbreviations and symbols
- Acknowledgments, preface, or foreword
- Body
  - Purpose of report—subject, scope, plan
  - Background
  - Policy statement
  - Introduction
  - Analysis and supporting data
  - Conclusions
  - Recommendations

- Glossary
- References
- Bibliography
- Appendices
- Index

Title Page

The title page should include:

- A title indicating the topic and the objective of the report (avoid using unfamiliar acronyms, and the self-evident phrase, "Report on ...")
- The writer's name
- The writer's organization
- The person or organization receiving the report
- The date

Letters

Include any letters authorizing or requesting the report and any letters of transmittal, as applicable.

Executive Summary

Any report of three or more pages must contain a short, informative overview. The executive summary, sometimes called a "management overview," "preliminary summary," or "abstract," is perhaps *the* most important element of the report because it might be the only part that is actually read. It states:

- The project's background
- The purpose and nature of the report
- The procedure for the study
- Budgetary implications
- Major findings and conclusions
- Recommendations

The key to a successful summary is to keep it short (200 to 250 words or less) and informative. The executive summary is important for several reasons:

- Busy managers can—and often do—read the summary and skim the rest of the report. It is aimed at managers and others who do not have the technical background or the time to read the entire report.
- The executive summary might be the basis for accepting or rejecting a report for publication or presentation.

- Executive summaries are the basis of computerized searches.

Executive summaries sometimes are placed immediately after the table of contents, though they usually appear after the title page and letters, if there are any. The following example of an executive summary comes from a scientific study that discusses research findings, conclusions, and recommendations.[1]

Sample Executive Summary

The City of Winslow hired McDuff, Inc., to perform a study of Wildwood Creek. The section of the creek that was studied is a one-mile-long area in Burns Nature Park, from Newell College to U.S. Highway 42. The study lasted seven months.

McDuff completed 13 tests on four different test dates. Wildwood scored fairly well on many of the tests, but there were some problem areas. For example, high levels of phosphates were uncovered in the water. The phosphates were derived from fertilizer or from animal and plant matter and waste. Also uncovered were small amounts of undesirable water organisms that are tolerant to pollutants and can survive in harsh environments.

McDuff recommends that (1) the tests done in this study be conducted two more times, through spring 2002; (2) other environmental tests be conducted, as listed in the conclusions and recommendations section; and (3) a voluntary cleanup of the creek be scheduled. With these steps, McDuff can better analyze the environmental integrity of Wildwood Creek.

Table of Contents

A well-organized, detailed table of contents makes it easy for the reader to identify all the elements in a document. Your table of contents should be a reliable road map that readers can follow to get through a process painlessly.

The table of contents should:

- Indicate the headings in the report, with their page numbers
- Include all items in the report except itself and the title page

The table of contents below is organized in a logical sequence for a discretionary grant program. The organization follows the order in which events occur and the order in which the public might ask questions about the program.[2]

Sample Table of Contents

Part 791: Javits Gifted and Talented Students

Subpart A: How the Grant Program Works

791.1 What is the Javits Gifted and Talented Students Education Program?

791.2 Am I eligible for a Javits Grant?

791.3 What activities are appropriate for Javits Grant funding?

791.4 What funding priorities may the Secretary establish?

791.5 What other regulations apply to the Javits Grant?

791.6 What definitions apply to the Javits Grant?

Subpart B: How to Apply for an Award

791.10 Where can I write to obtain a Javits Grant application?

791.11 What materials do I need to submit to be considered for a Javits Grant?

791.12 Where do I send my application?

791.13 When is my application due?

Subpart C: How the Secretary Makes an Award

791.20 How will the Secretary evaluate my application for a Javits Grant?

791.21 What selection criteria does the Secretary use to award Javits Grants?

791.22 Does the Secretary consider additional factors?

Subpart D: Grantees' Rights and Responsibilities

791.30 Under what conditions may I use my Javits Grant award?

791.31 What are my responsibilities for serving students and teachers in private schools?

List of Figures

Some writing experts recommend including a list of figures in reports with more than five illustrations (drawings, photographs, maps, charts, and graphs). The list of figures is a separate table of contents for the illustrations, which are numbered consecutively with Arabic numbers.

List of Tables

Some experts also recommend that a report with more than five tables contain a list of tables. This list is a separate table of contents for the tables, which are numbered consecutively with Arabic numbers.

List of Abbreviations and Symbols

This list is useful if a report contains many abbreviations and symbols that might confuse the reader. List each symbol and each abbreviation in alphabetical order and tell what it stands for.

Acknowledgments, Preface, and Foreword

Acknowledgments are an author's expression of indebtedness to all who helped with the report. This usually includes editors, proofreaders, advisors, and anyone who provided support or inspiration. The *preface* is written by the author and deals with the purpose, limitations, and scope of the report; it may also include acknowledgments if there is not a separate section for them. The *foreword* is written by someone other than the author or editor, usually someone eminent, and is included to lend credibility to the report.

Body

The body is the complete account of the topic, the part of a report that comes between the front matter just discussed and the back matter. It should cover the technical details and managerial implications. Technical documents often rely on three elements of form within the body: definitions, descriptions, and instructions.

The following are parts of the body:

- *Purpose.* This briefly presents the subject, scope, and organizational plan of the report.
- *Background.* This part of the report tells the reader how the report came to be written–the problems that led to it, the need for clarification of a subject, etc.
- *Policy statement.* If the report results from a specific public policy, that should be spelled out here.
- *Introduction.* The introduction deals with the subject of the report, supplementing and presenting the text.

You would normally include an introduction if you did not write a preface.

- *Analysis and supporting data.* In this section of the report, you analyze your findings and present information that supports your position. To persuade your readers, you must present concrete evidence to back up your position. Follow these guidelines:[3]
  - Introduce only enough data to prove each issue. Do not overwhelm your readers.
  - To be authoritative, be as concrete and specific as possible. Use numbers and percentages instead of such abstract phrases as "significant increase" or "substantial gain."
  - Provide quotes or opinions from respected sources.
  - Present tables and graphs.
- *Conclusions.* These are the deductions you draw from the data, your results. Your conclusions must prove your position by summarizing the implications of the data:
  - Does the analysis show that my conclusions are correct?
  - Are there factors that could affect the validity of my conclusions?

- *Recommendations.* Finally, you tell readers what they are expected to do to put your position into effect and what you, the writer, will do to further your position. Ask yourself:
  - Will my recommendations improve the current situation?
  - Do the advantages of my recommendations outweigh the disadvantages?
  - Are there reasonable alternatives to my recommendation(s), and should I present them?

Glossary

The glossary is an alphabetical listing of technical terms and their definitions, written in dictionary style. The terms selected will depend on the intended readers' background.

References

Any materials referred to or quoted from should be listed in a references section. References may take the form of:

- Footnotes (listed at the bottom of the page on which the reference appears)
- Endnotes (listed in a separate block section at the end of the chapter, section, or report)

In general, longer reports should have reference sections at the end of each section of the report.

Bibliography

The bibliography is a separate listing of all source materials used in researching the report but not cited in the text itself.

Appendices

Appendices contain information that supports or clarifies the report, but that is too detailed or voluminous to appear in the text without impeding the flow of ideas. This information might take the form of:

- Questionnaires used in the study
- Interviews used in the study
- Tabular results of the questionnaires and interviews
- Other data, presented in charts, graphs, and tables
- Correspondence

Appendices are especially useful when your report is going to a diverse audience, some of whom may not want or need to read the information in the appendix. Generally, each type of material should have its own appendix. Appendices are usually labeled "Appendix A," "Appendix B," and so on.

Index

The index is an alphabetical, cross-referenced list of all topics and subjects of importance in the report.

FORMATS FOR WORKPLACE REPORTS

The following sections explain how to organize the more common types of business reports, including:

- Research reports
- White papers
- Feasibility reports
- Progress reports
- Laboratory reports
- Test reports
- Trip reports
- Trouble reports
- Proposals
- Meeting minutes

Following a set format for a business report can help the reader identify your purpose early on and pay attention to your ideas, rather than to how you organized them.

Research Reports

Any research effort in the government is affected by the politics of the situation. You should not ignore political considerations, but you should take pains to conduct your research objectively and separately from politics. Research is a professional activity and should be kept professional. If you get personally involved in the outcome of a research project, you'll find research in the government terribly frustrating.

Judson Monroe offers the following guidelines for those who do government research and report writing:[4]

- *Make sure that your data are "clean"—that they can stand up to close scrutiny. Present and stand behind your data, but don't try to stretch the facts.*

- *Expect disagreement over your conclusions. Give others credit for the integrity of their opinions; in return, expect the same credit. Never take criticism personally.*

- *Make sure you know the politics of a situation before you try to collect data about it. Knowing what sort of political views you're going to run into will help you keep opinions separated from fact.*

- *Don't start drawing conclusions until you've obtained all the data you need—and all the data you set out to collect.*

- *Stay out of office politics. Don't get involved in any of the backstabbing and gossip that go on. This general good advice is especially critical to a researcher.*

- *When you get into your analysis of results, give at least brief coverage of all sides of any political argument.*

- *Whenever possible, leave decisions to those with the broadest possible point of view. Explain the options open to the decision makers, explain your point of view, and then leave major decisions to those with the overview.*

Monroe gives the following advice to managers and staff for each phase of the research/report-writing process (Figure 10-1):[5]

Figure 10-1 ◆ Tips for Writing Research Reports

Phase	Manager	Staff
• Brainstorming • Designing the research • Outlining	• Tell the researchers and writers everything you can about the nature of the assignment, audience, and subject. Make sure they understand the assignment. • Use contract process for the assignment. • To maintain the focus of the report, write the title for the staff.	• Make sure you thoroughly understand the assignment. • Brainstorm first, then collect data. • Brainstorm first, then narrow the scope of the assignment.
• Planning research • Collecting data	• To save money on research, help staff identify sources of existing data. • Post lists of existing data. • Require evaluation of alternative data sources. • Include time and money for a data source search.	• To help plan your statistical analysis, use data shells—graphs and charts without the numbers filled in. • Try to locate sources of existing data by talking to people in your agency, etc.
• Analyzing results	• Help staff keep the study in perspective. Assign at least one generalist to the research team. • Be sure to budget staff time for interpretation of data.	• Try to find someone outside the research team to help you maintain a broad perspective. • Consider the search for causes and recommendations a major part of the research effort.

Phase	Manager	Staff
• Assembling the final report	• Encourage staff to prepare complete outlines. • The manager is responsible for the entire review process and its consequences. If you want staff to do a professional job of getting the information you need to make decisions, you need to do a professional job review.	• Build paragraphs by starting with simple headline (topic) sentences, then add details, one sentence at a time in the correct order. • Review your own work carefully, using the standards you think management will use. • Note potential problems and ask about them. • To help ensure a quality report, seek and accept criticism from management.

Example—Planning a Research Project

The county council is running short of funds and is looking for ways to cut costs. The council is looking at the special reduced fees for senior citizens at two local golf courses. Should the county continue to give seniors this special rate? Determine the pros and cons of eliminating the reduced fees and recommend whether it should be done.

Answering the following questions might help you make a decision:

- How many senior citizens use the courses?
- How many take advantage of the reduced fee?
- How much revenue is lost because of the reduced fee?

- How many would stop using the course if the fees increased?
- How many feel that a fee increase would be fair?
- How many would be willing to pay extra voluntarily?
- What related programs could be changed to help make up the current revenue loss attributed to the reduced fee?

Data Sources for Government Research

Internal (in-house) *sources* include:

- Management information systems
- Personnel files, especially reports
- Budgets
- Expense records
- Travel records
- Time sheets
- Correspondence files
- Retirement, insurance, and Social Security records
- Minutes of meetings
- Intranet information

External sources include:

- Reports by other local, state, and federal agencies
- Reports from industry, trade journals, and corporate yearly statements
- Reports and files of community service organizations, such as the Chamber of Commerce, charity organizations, unions, fraternal organizations, foundations, and political parties
- Newspaper and magazine files (paper or online)
- University and college faculty studies
- Libraries
- Public records of marriage, health, parentage, age, welfare, place of business, property ownership and use, and taxation
- Census Bureau records
- Sales and inventory records
- Internet sites

Conducting the Research

Collect and document information carefully during the research stage. Make sure that you:

- Distinguish your summarizing from direct quotation.
- Include exact wording of direct quotations.
- Label the exact citation of the source (title, author, etc.).
- Carefully transfer information from notes to draft. Circle quotation marks to make it obvious what is quoted.
- Use the right citation system.

White Papers

The term "white paper" originated in the early 20th century in England. A white paper, or "command paper," referred to a parliamentary report, bound in a white cover, that laid out a government policy or proposed action.

Today's white papers are rarely bound. In fact, most are found on the Internet. Although white papers can come from companies, governments, or nonprofit organizations, they can be generally defined as communication tools used to explain something complex to an audience with little or no background on the topic.

Today the commercial white paper is the most common type of white paper. This report is used to explain technologies and products and show their benefits. Regardless of the source of white papers, people read them because they provide information and analysis regarding a problem they are facing.[6]

You might write a white paper for a number of reasons:

- To educate the public or an official on a complex subject
- To educate the media by providing the basis of an article
- To provide credibility on a given topic
- To redefine the way people view a given subject
- To answer a pressing question
- To explain a trend

How to Write a White Paper

The components of a white paper are the opening, the body, and the closing. In the opening, you state your purpose. In the body, you give (1) the benefits of dealing with the issue, (2) critical background information, (3) key considerations regarding your solution if you offer one, and (4) supporting evidence. In the closing you restate your purpose.

Although standards for white papers vary according to the industry or organization, some generalizations apply to almost all white papers (Figure 10-2):

Figure 10-2 ◆ White Paper Standards

Standard	Description
Length	White papers have an average length of 10 pages but can range from 5 to 20 or more.
Title	The title should be concise, informative, and appealing. Select a title that will make your audience want to read the paper.
Tone	Ideally, a white paper should have a neutral and informative tone. Some, however, contain a spin toward a given product or solution.
Illustrations	Well-written white papers include illustrations to help readers interpret the content of the paper.
Distribution	Most white papers are saved as PDF files so that they can be easily downloaded from the Internet. White papers can also be printed and distributed.
Time spent on the writing effort	Writing an effective white paper usually requires 6 to 8 weeks.

Feasibility Reports

A feasibility report explores the chances of success for a particular project, venture, or commitment. While a proposal usually recommends one solution, the feasibility report evaluates two or more possible solutions. The subject of such a report might be a move, the development of a new product or service, an expansion, or a major purchase. The feasibility report examines and compares alternatives, analyzes the pros and cons, and suggests which, if any, of the alternatives are feasible. It includes the following information:

- *A statement of purpose.* This statement is presented in the introduction to the report. For example, "The purpose of this report is to determine what type and how many new copiers the training office should purchase."

- *The problem.* This section gives background information on the problems or events leading up to the reports. For example, a feasibility report on new copiers would describe the wasted time and repair costs associated with the current copiers.

- *The scope.* The scope includes alternatives for accomplishing the purpose and the criteria by which each alternative will be examined, such as cost, personnel required, and legal or other special requirements. For example, the report on new copiers would give a list of the copiers being considered and discuss criteria (including the task, time, space, and cost requirements).

- *The alternatives under consideration.* This section gives a detailed evaluation of all alternatives under consideration. Normally, the evaluation of the pros and cons of each alternative (such as each type of copier) makes up a separate section of the report.

- *The conclusion.* The conclusion interprets and summarizes the evaluation of each alternative, usually in the order in which they are discussed in the body of the report.

- *The recommendation(s).* This section states the alternative that best meets the criteria according to the evaluation. For example, "Based on this evaluation, I recommend that we buy the XYZ copier for the training office."

Progress Reports

Progress reports, also known as status or activity reports, provide information about ongoing technical work and projects. Topics may include construction, expansion, or research and development. Progress reports are designed to keep management and clients informed about work in progress.

Because progress reports offer updated information on a topic with which the reader should already be familiar, the writer need not include statements of purpose, background, conclusions, and recommendations. Progress reports can be in the form of a memo or a letter. Regardless of format, they usually include the following information:

- Current projects
- Current problems
- Plans for the next period
- Staffing levels (current and required)

Sample Progress Report

To: John Rey, Comptroller
From: Linda James, Office Manager
Date: April 2, 2008
Subject: Reorganization of the Filing System

As you requested in your October 12 memo, I have completed plans for reorganizing and centralizing our filing system.

We will start work immediately, with Hollis White and Sandy Melendez supervising. Our principal objectives will be to:

- Establish a central filing department (with supplementary files where needed)
- Form an efficient messenger service to facilitate the flow of paper to and from the files

- Establish a sound and workable retention and disposition program for all records, reports, orders, and correspondence

We are convinced that these procedures will save us time and money by creating a highly efficient, smooth-flowing system.

I have notified department heads of this project and have asked them to assist us in the work that affects their departments. To keep the cost to a minimum and yet complete this work within the next five weeks, priority will be given to requests of those responsible for the success of this project.

I will submit a progress report to you at the end of the second week.

Laboratory Reports

A laboratory report communicates information obtained from a laboratory test or investigation. It is longer and more formal than a test report. A laboratory report states:

- The reason for the investigation
- The conditions, equipment, and procedures for testing
- Any problems encountered
- Conclusions reached
- Recommendations based on the conclusions

Each laboratory usually establishes the organization of its reports. The laboratory reports often emphasize equipment and procedures because these factors can be critical in determining the accuracy of the data.

Sample Laboratory Report[7]

LABORATORY REPORT
BOREHOLE FOSSIL SAMPLES
BRAINTREE CREEK SITE, WEST VIRGINIA

INTRODUCTORY SUMMARY

Last week you sent us six fossil samples from the Braintree Creek site. Having analyzed the samples in our lab, we believe they suggest the presence of coal-bearing rock. As you requested, this report will give a summary of the materials and procedures we used in this project, along with any problems we had.

As you know, our methodology is to identify microfossils in the samples, estimate the age of the rock by when the microfossils existed, and then make assumptions about whether the surrounding rock might contain coal.

LAB MATERIALS

Our lab analysis relies on only one piece of specialized equipment: a Piketon electron microscope. Besides the Piketon, we use a simple 400-power manual microscope. Other equipment is similar to that included in any basic geology lab, such as filtering screens and burners.

LAB PROCEDURE

Once we receive a sample, we first try to identify the kinds of microfossils the rocks contain. Our specific lab procedure for your samples consisted of two steps:

Step 1

We used a 400-power microscope to visually classify the microfossils that were present. Upon inspection of the samples, we concluded that there were two main types of microfossils: nannoplankton and foraminifera.

Step 2

Next, we had to extract the microfossils from the core samples you provided. We used two different techniques:

Nannoplankton Extraction Technique

- Selected a pebble-sized piece of the sample
- Thoroughly crushed the piece under water
- Used a dropper to remove some of the material that floats to the surface (It contains the nannoplankton)
- Dried the nannoplankton-water combination
- Placed the nannoplankton on a slide

Foraminifera Extraction Technique

- Boiled a small portion of the sample
- Used a microscreen to remove clay and other unwanted material
- Dried the remaining material (foraminifera)
- Placed foraminifera on a slide

PROBLEMS ENCOUNTERED

The entire lab procedure went as planned. The only problem was minor and occurred when we removed one of the samples from its shipping container. As the bag was taken from the shipping box, it broke open. The sample shattered when it fell onto the table. Fortunately, we had an extra sample from the same location.

CONCLUSION

Judging from the types of fossils present in the sample, we believe they come from rocks of an age that might contain coal. This conclusion is based on limited testing; so we suggest that you test more samples at the site. We would be glad to help with additional sampling and testing.

I will call you this week to discuss our study and any possibility of follow-up you may wish us to do.

Sincerely,
Joseph Rappaport, Senior Geologist

Test Reports

Test reports are informal, and usually internal, reports on specific tests. They may report the results of a test, or a problem encountered with a test. They may take the format of a memo or letter, depending on whether the intended reader is internal or external to the organization. Typically, test reports include the following information:

- The test's purpose
- Problems with the test (if applicable)
- Conditions and procedures for testing (if such information is of use or interest to the reader)
- Results and, sometimes, the significance of the results

- Conclusions
- Recommendations

Trip Reports

A trip report discusses the accomplishments and findings of an employee's business trip. It establishes a permanent record from which other employees can learn. As internal reports, trip reports usually take the memo report format. They contain the following information:

- Purpose of the trip
- Major events
- Conclusions
- Actions taken
- Recommendations

Trouble Reports

Trouble reports deal with incidents that interfere with normal activity, such as accidents, equipment failures, communication breakdowns, unplanned work stoppages, and damage from fire, flood, or storms. They enable managers to determine the cause of a problem and make the changes necessary to prevent its recurrence. Typically, trouble reports use a memo format and contain the following information:

- Description of the problem (who, what, when, where, why, and how)
- Resulting injuries or deaths
- Resulting damage
- Costs (in terms of lost work, equipment damage, worker's compensation awards, or lawsuits)
- Witnesses
- Any action taken (including treatment of injuries)
- Recommendations (such as training, equipment improvements, protective clothing, and so on)

Because trouble reports might be used as evidence in lawsuits, it is important to:

- Include precise times, dates, locations, treatment of injuries, names of witnesses, and any other crucial information
- Avoid making statements of condemnation or blame
- Avoid making definite statements about the cause

Proposals

A proposal is a document that attempts to persuade the reader to follow a plan or course of action. Though a proposal can be internal or external, government proposals are almost always internal.

Internal Proposals

An internal proposal, or issue paper, is a document written for others within an organization. It suggests a change or improvement. Quite often, such proposals seek approval for a capital expenditure; therefore, persuasion is a primary purpose of these documents.

Typically, internal proposals take the memo report format and contain the following information:

- Background leading to the problem – Describe how the problem developed, its effects, and any efforts made to solve it
- Proposal for fixing the problem
- Arguments in favor of the proposed solution. You'll need to describe the benefits for your reader, using supporting evidence. These might include any of the following:
  - Results of experiments

  - Definitions
  - Comparisons
  - Required equipment, materials, and personnel
  - Quotes
  - Proposed schedule
  - Expert testimony
  - Statistics
  - Reasons
  - Examples

- Opposing arguments and rebuttals. You can understand and address opposing arguments through research, discussion, and feedback. Ask a person who is opposed to your proposal to give his or her viewpoint. Then think of ways to refute the arguments.
- Request for action. Let your readers know clearly what steps they need to take.
- Conclusion that restates recommendations and offers other information or assistance.

Sample Internal Proposal[8]

As you requested, I have evaluated our present accounting system. I recommend that we upgrade our software in accordance with the attached specifications. The software will provide us with advanced accounting software functions like accounting journal entries, accounting transaction ledgers, dynamic account numbers, bank accounts, check writing, and reconciliation.

This upgrade will (1) save time and (2) reduce errors. As soon as I receive your approval, I will contact DataHelp and set up a schedule for the modifications.

Time Savings

The proposed upgrade will reduce the time required to do monthly reconciliations by 15 percent. In addition, we will be able to prepare quarterly reports in approximately half the time now required.

Reduction in Errors

We will not need to enter business data in each program we use. We can enter it once and have the data shared across programs like Microsoft Office Word and Excel. This capability will reduce errors. Furthermore, our quarterly reports will be more accurate because the software modifications will provide additional cross-checking to further reduce errors.

Because of the time savings and reduction in errors, we should immediately implement this upgrade.

External Proposals

An external proposal is written for a reader outside the writer's organization. An example of an external proposal is a response to a request for proposals (RFP) issued by an organization seeking new equipment or services.

The format for external proposals is usually very structured and formal. Public grants usually require full proposals that range from 15 to 100 pages and contain such sections as a cover letter, title page, abstract, introduction, need/problem, objectives, methods, evaluation, dissemination, budget, and appendices.

Meeting Minutes

As the official record of meetings, minutes must be accurate, complete, and clear. Someone who is not responsible for running or facilitating the meeting should take the minutes.

The Importance of Minutes

Recording meeting minutes is important for several reasons, including:

- Minutes provide a written record—evidence that the meeting took place and addressed issues, actions, and decisions
- They are a reminder and a useful follow-up tool for actions and decisions
- Minutes provide an efficient way to prepare the agenda for the next meeting
- They inform those who did not attend the meeting about what occurred

Once minutes are formally approved in an meeting, they can even serve as evidence in a court of law.

Guidelines for Writing and Distributing Minutes

The following are some useful guidelines for writing and distributing minutes:

1. If you have a well-written agenda, use it as a guide.

2. Use headings and a consistent format. Headings may include the date, objectives, attendees, topics, decisions, and action items, for example.

3. Include only a summary of the discussion, highlighting the major points. Give people credit for their ideas without inserting opinion or judgmental comments.

4. Provide relevant, specific details on the important topics.

5. Provide complete names and titles.

6. Highlight action items, persons responsible, and deadlines. Then attendees will understand their commitments.

7. Complete and distribute draft minutes as soon as possible. Every day that goes by without minutes, you risk "memory loss."

8. If there are significant disputes about information contained in the minutes, try to resolve the concerns with key participants and, if necessary, issue revised minutes.

9. Issue final versions of the minutes to all meeting attendees (with copies to appropriate files).

What Minutes Include

Minutes typically include:

- Agenda
- Main objectives
- Critical discussion points
- Overheads or data presented
- Agreements and disagreements
- Decisions
- Recommendations
- Issues for further discussion
- Action items (with timeline and persons responsible for each action item)

Sample Meeting Minutes

DATE: March 24, 2007

FROM: Dr. Jody Harris

TO: Dr. Erica Baldwin, Dr. Valerie Brook, Dr. Kim Chin, Mr. William Cohen, Mr. William Johnston, Dr. James Lee, Dr. Juan Mesa, Dr. Anne Phillips, Ms. Susan Powell, Dr. Derek Smith, Ms. Jonique Thompson

SUBJECT: Minutes of Type B Meeting with Beta Biologics

Meeting Date: March 22, 2007

Location: Conference Room 4, Building A

Meeting Requestor/Sponsor: Beta Biologics

Type of Meeting: Type B

FDA Meeting Leader: Dr. Juan Mesa

Recorder: Dr. Jody Harris

FDA Attendees: Dr. Derek Smith, Dr. Anne Phillips, Dr. Juan Mesa, Mr. William Johnston, Dr. Valerie Brook, Dr. Jody Harris

Sponsor Attendees: Mr. William Cohen, Dr. Erica Baldwin, Ms. Jonique Thompson, Dr. James Lee

Meeting Objectives:

1. Comparison of the two interpretations of toxicity reports and resolution of differences.
2. Discussion of whether to grant a request that the FDA allow a pharmacokinetic study for Beta Biologics' product to begin in normal, healthy volunteers.
3. Clarification of the FDA's requirements for demonstrating comparability between the old product and the new product.

Page 2

Discussion Points:

- Differences in toxicity reports: how they occurred and which report is reliable.
- Pros and cons of allowing a pharmacokinetic study for Beta Biologics' product to begin in normal, healthy volunteers.
- Requirements for demonstrating comparability between the old product and the new product.

Decisions/Agreements Reached:

- The December 2006 toxicity report is not valid because of statistical error. The calculations of toxin levels were incorrect and reflected lower levels than actually occurred.
- Beta Biologics must recalculate toxin levels and submit the results.
- The FDA will allow a pharmacokinetic study for Beta Biologics' product to begin in normal, healthy volunteers.
- It was decided that, subject to approval by Dr. Smith, the new biologic must be tested under the following conditions:
  - Subjects must be between the ages of 18 and 45.
  - Each subject must receive a thorough medical examination before being allowed into the program.

Issues Requiring Further Discussion: How to prevent statistical error in the future.

Action Items: Dr. Harris will check with Dr. Smith (Division Director) by March 25 for final approval of the conditions for testing. Dr. Harris will notify Dr. Baldwin of the Division Director's decision.

Attachments/Handouts: November 2006 and December 2006 toxicity reports.

TEST YOURSELF

THE REPORT'S TONE

Rewrite the following report to give it a more personal tone and make it more interesting to read.

Bennett County Hospital
Preliminary Report 2
June 16, 2007

Submitted to the Board of Trustees
by the Review Committee

This report is the second in a series of three which the Board of Trustees has requested for its study of feasibility of the proposed expansion of the Bennett County Hospital facilities. The third report of this committee will be submitted in three months' time and will contain the data requested in the Board's letter of December 2, 2006.

General Information

Bennett County Hospital has received full accreditation from the highest national authority on hospital accreditation, the Joint Commission on Accreditation of Hospitals—the first time that such accreditation has been granted by the Commission.

It can be concluded that this full accreditation is a result of the fact that the hospital meets or exceeds high professional standards in terms of its personnel as well as its physical plant and special services.

This committee ascertained that certain steps had been taken in the past year that have enhanced the hospital's quality of service provided. Intensive care facilities were significantly upgraded. Following completion of a comparative study, nurses' salaries were increased in order to maintain a well-qualified nursing staff. Furthermore, it has been the decision of the hospital to institute the holding of monthly meetings through which the cooperation of staff, administration, and trustees can be maintained . . . .

See the Appendix for suggested revisions.

A report is an impartial, objective, planned presentation of facts. It should be logical, accurate, reliable, and easy to read. Though generally not as conversational as a letter, a report should nonetheless be friendly and professional.

The three parts of an informal report are the opening, unfolding, and conclusion. A formal report may also include an executive summary, table of contents, and appendices.

Following a set format for a business report—whether informal or formal—helps the reader to identify your purpose early on and pay attention to your ideas, rather than to how you organized them. Each type of report has a specific purpose. Research reports must be kept separate from politics and should present all sides of an argument. Internal proposals are documents written for others within an organization that suggest a change or improvement; external proposals are written for readers outside the writer's organization. A proposal typically recommends one solution, whereas a feasibility report usually evaluates two or more possible solutions.

Progress reports, laboratory reports, test reports, trip reports, and trouble reports are all common in the workplace. Each conveys specific information relevant to a project or function.

Finally, the minutes of a meeting constitute an official record of proceedings and therefore must be accurate, complete, and clear.

NOTES

1 William S. Pfeiffer, *Pocket Guide to Technical Writing* (Upper Saddle River, NJ: Prentice Hall, 1998), 152. Used with permission.
2 Plain Language Action and Information Network, "Writing Reader-Friendly Documents." Online at www.plainlanguage.gov (accessed November 2007), 10–11.
3 Padraic Spence, *Write Smart: The Complete Guide to Business Writing* (Great Barrington, MA: North River Press, 1996), 27.
4 Judson Monroe, *Effective Research and Report Writing in Government* (New York: McGraw-Hill, 1980), 6–7.
5 Ibid.
6 Wikipedia, The Free Encyclopedia, "White paper," Wikimedia Foundation, Inc. Online at http://en.wikipedia.org/wiki/White_paper (accessed January 2008).
7 William S. Pfeiffer, *Pocket Guide to Technical Writing* (Upper Saddle River, NJ: Prentice Hall, 1998), 137–138. Used with permission.
8 Adapted from Padraic Spence, *Write Smart: The Complete Guide to Business Writing* (Great Barrington, MA: North River Press, 1996), 32. Used with permission.

CHAPTER 11

Achieving Skill in Technical Writing

◆ Technically Speaking . . . ◆

"How's the technical writing class going?" Maria asked Tom during his break.

"Okay. Our assignment for next class is to write some information for a safety manual. I'm not sure how to do that, but I have a copy of one from the Centers for Disease Control. It seems very clear, so I might model mine after it. Here's a description of respiratory protection equipment, for example."

D. Respiratory Protection

Respiratory hazards may occur through exposure to harmful dusts, fogs, fumes, mists, gases, smoke, sprays, and vapors. The best means of protecting personnel is through the use of engineering controls, e.g., local exhaust ventilation. Only when engineering controls are not practical or applicable shall respiratory protective equipment be employed to reduce personnel exposure.

The Office of Health and Safety is responsible for the Respiratory Protection Program at CDC. Workers requiring the use of respirators must first obtain medical approval from the Occupational Health Clinic physician to wear a respirator before a respirator can be issued. The Industrial Hygiene Section conducts respirator training and fit tests and is responsible for determining the proper type of respiratory protection required for the particular hazard.

Adherence to the following guidelines will help ensure the proper and safe use of respiratory equipment:

- *Wear only the respirator you have been instructed to use. For example, do not wear a self-containing breathing apparatus if you have been assigned and fitted for a half-mask respirator.*
- *Wear the correct respirator for the particular hazard. For example, some situations, such as chemical spills or other emergencies, may require a higher level of protection than your respirator can handle. Also, the proper cartridge must be matched to the hazard. (A cartridge designed for dusts and mists will not provide protection for chemical vapors.)*
- *Check the respirator for a good fit before each use. Positive and negative fit checks should be conducted.*
- *Check the respirator for deterioration before and after use. Do not use a defective respirator.*
- *Recognize indications that cartridges and canisters are at their end of service. If in doubt, change the cartridges or canisters before using the respirator.*
- *Practice moving and working while wearing the respirator so that you can get used to it.*
- *Clean the respirator after each use, thoroughly dry it, and place the cleaned respirator in a sealable plastic bag.*
- *Store respirators carefully in a protected location away from excessive heat, light, and chemicals.*

"What do you think?" Tom asked.

"It seems very clear. Even nontechnical people could understand it," said Maria.

"That's the whole idea," Tom responded.

Technical writing involves writing, editing, and publishing information related to technology, medicine, engineering, science, or a similar field.

We can distinguish technical writing from other types of writing by its:

- Writer
- Purpose
- Style
- Subject matter

One major difference between technical and other types of writing is the role of the *writer*. Unlike business documents, which are usually written by one person, technical documents are often the result of collaboration among the writer, subject matter expert, editor, and others.

The *purpose* of technical writing is to inform, instruct, describe, explain, or otherwise document scientific or industrial processes and mechanisms.[1]

Because the primary purpose of technical and business writing is to convey information accurately, the *style* of business and technical writing is utilitarian. The writer is not concerned with painting word pictures or dazzling the reader with new and daring visions. The focus is on the information. The technical writer aims to convey information as clearly, completely, and concisely as possible.

Technical writers deal with specific, factual *subject matter* related to engineering, computers and other technology, and physical, biological, and social sciences. Technical writing is concerned with objects, processes, systems, or abstract ideas. The focus is on describing and explaining. The reader should be able to take away knowledge about how something works or how to do something. In addition to the types of technical writing discussed in this chapter, many white papers and some laboratory reports could be considered technical writing.

THE AUDIENCE FOR TECHNICAL WRITING

Technical documents are generally intended for many readers. The readers might be technical professionals, non-technical managers, or general readers. Technical writing should be targeted to the reader's technical proficiency and understanding. Often, the technical writer is writing for an audience with a diverse background. Some readers might know a great deal about the topic and might be bored or insulted by writing that spells out what they already know. Readers who know less about the topic might be confused by complex content. To make your writing appropriate to your audience:

- *Define the audience.* Who will read this document? What kind of background and education do they have? What kinds of functions do they perform? Why will they read this? What terms will they need to have defined? What jargon do they commonly use?

- *Write for the majority, while accommodating minorities.* When writing for a mixed audience of technical and nontechnical people, include enough data to satisfy the technical readers, while also describing the data in terms that lay readers can understand. Use the "gist" test: Nontechnical readers should be able to get the gist of your ideas.

- *When the primary audience is nontechnical, flesh out explanations.* When introducing new terms, include a separate sentence or paragraph defining them.

- *When the primary audience is technical, include parenthetical explanations.* These serve as quick refreshers.

- *Put yourself in your readers' place and ask the questions they would ask.* Try asking "Who?" "What?"

"Where?" "When?" "Why?" and "How?" A reader assembling a swing set, for example, might ask:

- What tools do I need?
- Where should it be placed (grass, sand, acceptable slope)?
- Who can use it (weight and height restrictions)?
- How do I assemble it?

Carol M. Barnum and Saul Carliner share the following information about audiences for writers of technical documents (Figure 11-1):[2]

Figure 11-1 ◆ Readers of Technical Communication

What research tells us about audience	What technical writers should do
• People decide how much attention to pay to a document, based on the product, the packaging, and the document's level of difficulty.	• Minimize the amount of reading required. • Consider how readers will use the document and organize and design it accordingly.

<table>
<tr><th>What research tells us about audience</th><th>What technical writers should do</th></tr>
<tr><td>• Readers use documents as tools. Sullivan and Flowers discovered that, in using a library manual:
– No one carefully read more than two sentences at a time.
– Most people began to use the product before they turned to the manual.
– People used the manual only when they were not successful in achieving their goal.
– Most did not read the introduction first.
– Most did not read any section in its entirety.</td><td>• Make the table of contents and index match topics people are looking for.
• Design pages for easy skimming and scanning.
• Use structures such as numbers and lists of steps to help readers.</td></tr>
<tr><td>• Readers actively interpret documents as they read.</td><td>• Use active voice and action-verb sentences with people or organizations as subjects of the sentences.</td></tr>
<tr><td>• Readers interpret documents in light of their own knowledge and expectations.</td><td>• Provide clear organization.
• Follow the given-new contract: Present information in a framework of what readers already know or have been given.
• Maintain coherence and consistency by using:
– headings, listings, changes in typography, and page placement to show organization
– chunks, or small, visually distinct sections of information
– hierarchical organization of information (queuing)
• Provide multiple pathways through a document by using a combination of words and pictures to give information.</td></tr>
</table>

TECHNICAL DEFINITIONS

In technical writing it is important to specify meaning. A word or phrase can mean one thing in everyday speech and quite another when it relates to technology. For example, a "chord" is a combination of tones sounded at the same time, but it is also a straight line joining two points on a curve. The technical writer must understand the correct meaning for the technology and make sure the reader does as well.

Technical definitions can be classified into three categories:

- Informal or parenthetical
- Formal
- Extended

Informal or Parenthetical Definitions

An informal definition explains a term by giving a familiar word or phrase as a synonym. For example:

- "This is a discrete, or distinct, step in the process."

Sometimes, informal definitions are included in parentheses immediately after the word they define. For example:

- "This process includes 10 discrete (distinct and separate) steps."

Formal Definitions

Formal definitions are generally one to three sentences. A formal definition should include the following:

- The term
- The category in which the term is classified
- Unique features of the term compared with other terms or elements in the category

For example:

- "A mastiff [term] is a large dog [category] with a short, fawn-colored coat [distinguishing features]."

Extended Definitions

For a more complex term or a term with a very specific meaning, a technical writer might extend the definition through:

- Example
- Analogy
- Analysis

Example

Using specific examples gives the reader details useful in forming a mental picture. For example:

- "A diphthong is a single speech sound that begins with one vowel sound and moves to another in the same syllable, such as 'oi' in 'coil.'"

Analogy

Using an analogy involves noting a correspondence between two otherwise unlike things. For example:

- "A disk pack is a computer storage device consisting of several magnetic disks that can be used and stored as a unit. Like a jukebox, it sorts the stored disks, allowing the operator to choose the disk containing the desired information."

Analysis

Figure 11-2 summarizes techniques for analyzing definitions:

Figure 11-2 ◆ Analyzing Definitions

Technique	Example
Explaining the term's causes	Malaria is an infectious disease marked by cycles of chills, fever, and sweating. It is associated with humid, tropical climates because it is transmitted by the bite of the female anopheles mosquito.
Breaking down the definition into component parts, with a definition of each component part	Fire is the visible heat energy released from the rapid oxidation of a fuel. . . . The elements necessary to create fire [are] oxygen, heat, and burnable material or fuel. Air provides sufficient oxygen for combustion; the intensity of the heat needed to start a fire depends on the characteristics of the burnable material or fuel. A burnable substance is one that will sustain combustion after an initial application of heat to start it.
Explaining the term's origins	"Dismal," which means gloomy or depressing, comes from the Latin dies mali ("evil days").

Rules for Definitions

Figure 11-3 summarizes some techniques for writing clear definitions:

Figure 11-3 ◆ Writing Clear Definitions

Rule	Instead of	Try
State definitions positively.	"A condition that is endemic is not rare."	"An endemic condition is widespread in a particular area or among particular people."
Avoid defining a term by restating it.	"Iridescence occurs when an object becomes iridescent."	"Iridescence is a state in which objects produce an array of rainbow-like colors.
Avoid "is when" and "is where." Instead, tell *what* the term is.	"An ion is when an atom acquires a net of electric charge."	"An ion is an atom, group of atoms, or molecule that has acquired a net electric charge."
Avoid or explain terms unfamiliar to your readers.	"Pizzicato means plucking with the fingers instead of using a bow."	"Pizzicato means playing a stringed instrument, such as a violin, by plucking the strings instead of drawing a bow across them."

MECHANICAL DESCRIPTIONS

To develop a mechanism description:

- Explain the mechanism's purpose and general operating standards.
  - What is the mechanism's main use?
  - Where is the mechanism used?

  - How often does the mechanism operate, and for how long?
  - What conditions must be met before the mechanism can be operated? (For example, some mechanisms work only at certain temperature or humidity levels.)
  - To what extent do people control the mechanism, directly or indirectly?

- Visually describe the mechanism as a whole.
  - Give its general size and dimensions.
  - Compare its shape to that of related mechanisms.
- Describe the principles of the mechanism's operation.
  - How does the mechanism work?
  - What are the major components? (Note the number of features and the relative size of each.)
- List and describe all parts of the mechanism.
  - List each specific part.
  - Show drawings or photos of parts—at least the parts your readers might not recognize.

– Explain how each part functions in relation to other parts.

– Explain where each part is located.

– Explain how each part functions.

TEST YOURSELF

WRITING A MECHANISM DESCRIPTION

Using the guidelines above, write a description of a computer mouse. See the Appendix for a suggested description.

TECHNICAL INSTRUCTIONS

Most of us have had the experience of trying unsuccessfully to follow directions. Maryann Piotrowski underlines the importance of simple, clear instructions:

> *Though seemingly a simple task, writing clear instructions demands careful thought and execution. Every step must be delineated, every doubt clarified, every risk defined. Whether a set of directions is a formal document that will be included in a procedures manual or an informal note explaining how to get to the new plant, it should be simple and clear.*[3]

Like mechanical descriptions, technical instructions help the reader understand how a process or mechanism works. Technical instructions must also show the reader how he or she can perform a process. Typical processes for which instructions are required include:

- Operating
- Maintaining
- Repairing
- Assembling
- Testing

To write technical instructions:

1. State the purpose of the instructions.
2. List the conditions that must be met before beginning the operation (such as equipment and skill requirements, climate conditions, and time restraints).
3. Give the sequence of instructions.

Tips for making instructions easier to understand include:

- Divide the process into short, simple steps. (Steps in washing a car might include wetting the car, mixing soap with water, applying soapy water to the car, scrubbing, rinsing, drying with soft towels, applying wax, and buffing.)

- Use familiar terms. Don't frustrate your reader. Use language everyone can understand.

- Use bulleted or numbered lists whenever possible. Use numbers to show the order in which steps are to be performed.

- Label all steps with numbers or words that indicate sequence (such as "first," "second," "next," "then"). If two operations must be performed simultaneously, be sure to make this clear. For example, "While holding the Control key, press the F4 key."

- Be concise, but don't confuse the reader by leaving out too many articles ("a," "an," and "the") or explanatory phrases.

- Move from the familiar to the unfamiliar. Relate what the readers don't know to what they do know.

- Reassure the reader. Insert occasional phrases that tell readers when they are proceeding correctly. (For example, "If you have completed this step properly, the green light will flash when you push the red button.")

- Give all necessary warnings. Explain all conditions under which an operation should or should not be performed. (For example, "CAUTION: Do not operate the equipment during electrical storms.")

- Explain the reasons for performing a step. This will help readers understand the process and complete the step correctly.

- Use decision tables ("if-then" tables) if the user must make a decision. Figure 11-4 offers a sample if-then table:

Figure 11-4 ◆ Sample If-Then Table

If	Then
The indicator light is green	Press the toggle switch
The indicator light is yellow	Release the brake
The indicator light is red	Remove the jam from the feeder belt
The light is not on	Check the plug in the wall socket

- Include visual aids. Use simple drawings or diagrams to explain a process or mechanism more clearly than words. Make sure the visual aids are simple and clearly labeled. (See Chapter 6 for information about flow charts, which are an excellent tool for describing technical procedures.)

- Test the instructions. Have someone unfamiliar with the process follow the instructions so you can determine where they are confusing or unclear. Revise any problem areas and retest your instructions.[4]

The following example is a process description from the "Help" function of Microsoft® Word (2000) that uses a numerical list:[5]

HOW TO: Print Envelopes or Labels from a List of Addresses in Word 2000

1. On the Tools menu, click Envelopes and Labels, and then click the Envelopes tab.
2. In the Delivery address box, do one of the following:
   - Enter or edit the mailing address.
   - Insert a mailing address from an electronic address book.
3. In the Return address box, you can accept the default return address or do one of the following:
   - Enter or edit the return address.
   - Insert a return address from an electronic address book.
   - Omit a return address by selecting the Omit check box.
4. To select an envelope size, the type of paper feed, and other options, click Options.
5. In the Envelopes and Labels dialog box, do one of the following:
   - To print the envelope now, insert an envelope in the printer as shown in the Feed box, and then click Print.
   - To attach the envelope to the current document for later editing or printing, click Add To Document.
   - To modify an existing envelope that's already attached to the current document, click Change Document.

The following are samples from the "before" and "after" versions of NASA's safety handbook.[6] The original manual was written in legalese, was poorly organized, and mixed administrative and technical material. The new handbook has been streamlined and written in a user-friendly question-and-answer format. Each chapter begins with "Who must follow this chapter?" so employees no longer have to wade through irrelevant introductory material to find the information they need.

Sample Procedure

BEFORE

Cryogenic Materials
Chapter 204
204.1 Purpose

The purpose of this chapter is to provide minimum safety requirements for the safe handling and use of the more commonly used cryogenic substances and to identify specific precautions, emergency treatment (Attachment 204A, Appendix B), protective clothing and equipment guidelines, training requirements, and housekeeping information.

Requirements set forth in this chapter shall apply to all JSC personnel performing operations that require the use, handling, or storage of cryogenic materials. Liquid oxygen or liquid hydrogen used as propellants shall follow the requirements of chapter 206, "Explosives and Propellants."

Each supervisor involved with cryogenic substances shall thoroughly understand the hazards involved, the safe handling methods, work procedures, and emergency procedures, and ensure that these procedures are understood and strictly adhered to.

Facility managers shall be familiar with the cryogenic safety and emergency procedures to ensure that they are implemented in the workplace.

Each employee working with cryogenic substances shall thoroughly understand the hazards involved, safe handling methods, work procedures, and emergency procedures.

AFTER

This could be you . . .

Two technicians passed out while transferring liquid nitrogen from a truck because nitrogen spilled into the loading dock and displaced oxygen in the area. They were rescued and are okay. A liquid helium dewar ruptured. Fortunately, no one was in the room at the time. A liquid nitrogen dewar exploded and sent glass fragments flying. Fortunately, the technicians working with the dewar were not in the path of the flying glass.

You must follow this chapter if you:

a. Handle, store, or transfer cryogenic liquids as a part of your job.

b. Handle or work around gaseous nitrogen, oxygen, or hydrogen.

c. Supervise anyone who does the above tasks.

FORMS OF TECHNICAL WRITING

Many of the types of reports described in Chapter 10 are used for technical writing, including feasibility reports, status/progress reports, test reports, trip reports, trouble reports, technical formal reports, and technical proposals. In addition, technical writing is used in developing:

- Technical manuals
- Journal articles
- Abstracts
- Specifications
- Online help systems
- Computer-based training (CBT)
- Web-based training (WBT)

Technical Manuals

Technical manuals are documents written to help technical and nontechnical readers use and maintain equipment. Common types of manuals include:

- Installation manuals
- Instruction and users' manuals
- Maintenance manuals
- Operations manuals—theoretical information about how equipment operates
- Sales manuals—information about specifying and purchasing equipment

Operations and users' manuals should be written for a general, nontechnical audience. Manuals make extensive use of technical descriptions and instructions. Illustrations, especially labeled diagrams, will help nontechnical users locate parts as they are discussed.

Installation and maintenance manuals, on the other hand, are meant primarily for the highly technical expert who installs, repairs, and maintains a piece of equipment. They rely heavily on tools like schematics and exploded diagrams.

Format for Technical Manuals

Maintenance manuals are usually written for the person who repairs and maintains a piece of equipment. The reader might be highly skilled or semiskilled. Illustrations might include schematic diagrams, blueprints, tables of operating data, performance curves, and specifications. A general format for a maintenance manual is:

- Title/cover page
- Preface/introduction
- Table of contents
- Mechanism descriptions
- Process descriptions

- User instructions
- Appendices
- Glossary
- Index

Guidelines for Technical Manuals

Gary Blake and Robert Bly offer general guidelines for writing better manuals:[7]

- *Remember that manual writing is instruction writing. Practice by writing instructions for nontechnical activities.*
- *Be complete. It is better to assume too little knowledge, experience, and familiarity with your technology on the part of the reader than to assume too much.*
- *Be clear and correct.*
- *Be unambiguous. It is better to be repetitious and perfectly clear than brief and possibly unclear.*
- *Set off warnings from the rest of the text using special typefaces. Boldface critical warnings and put them in boxes. Italicize or underline secondary warnings.*

- *Use the imperative voice—"Connect the cables" is better than "The cables should be connected."*

Steps in Creating a Technical Manual

The following steps are useful for creating a manual:

1. Prepare a documentation plan.

2. Complete an audience analysis and use it for content, design, layout, and text.

3. Brainstorm and mind map (see Chapter 2).

4. Complete a task analysis.

   Elements of a task analysis include:

   - The performer—the person completing the task
   - The action—the work in the task (verb and noun)
   - The environment—atmosphere and conditions under which the performer must complete the action, including performer's attitude and emotions
   - The goal—what the action will achieve
   - Requirements—tools, knowledge, or experience the performer must have

- Your assumptions—things you will take for granted (e.g., I assume the reader will know how to turn on the machine)

Steps in completing a task analysis are:

1. Select a task.
2. Divide the task into actions.
3. Define each action's goal.
4. List the action's performer.
5. List the starting conditions (including any previously completed actions).
6. List the requirements.
7. List your assumptions.
8. Describe the environment.

5. Complete an audience-task matrix.
   - List all members of your audience on one axis.
   - List every task you have analyzed on the other axis.
   - Note which tasks apply to each audience member.

6. Establish formats for layout and writing.

Journal Articles

Publishing an article in a trade or professional journal offers many advantages:

- Demonstrates your expertise to others in your field, enhancing your professional standing
- Provides good publicity for your organization
- Allows you to contribute to the pool of technical knowledge
- Provides an opportunity for you to learn more about the subject on which you are writing

Although being published in a journal is prestigious, it is not impossible. There are more than 6,000 business, technical, academic, scientific, and trade publications in the United States. These journals are aimed at specialized audiences of professionals with knowledge and experience in a particular field, and journal editors are always interested in concise, well-written, relevant articles. Topics include case studies, trends, new ideas and products, technological advances, improvements in manufacturing techniques, research findings, and experiments.

The keys to an effective journal article are a clear purpose and good organization. Outlining the article is critical to getting it published. The subject must be in accordance with the journal's specific subject matter, and the article must present new and interesting information for its readers.

When you're preparing to write a journal article, follow these steps:

1. *Evaluate the topic.* What new contributions can you make to the field? Why are your ideas worth publishing?

2. *Evaluate the effort.* What kind of work will be required to research, organize, draft, and edit the article? Is publication worth the time and effort?

3. *Identify relevant journals.* Many journals are published by professional societies and organizations. A little research can help you identify journals that might be interested in your topic.

4. *Research relevant journals.* Once you have narrowed your list to a few possible journals, find out more about each. How many readers does it have? What are those readers' interests? Does it have a good reputation? Are articles from it cited in other works? Does your article relate to the journal's goals?

5. *Determine the journals' requirements.* From your research, you should be able to narrow your list of journals to one or two. Contact each journal to find out

what it requires in terms of style, tone, length, and format. (Many journals provide author's guidelines to prospective authors.) Review some back issues to get a feel for style and content.

6. *Write and submit the article.* Remember, the journal's editors may (and probably will) edit your work. However, they will want to start with a manuscript that conforms to their guidelines and is clear, concise, and well written.

7. *Read it and reap the rewards of authorship.*

Abstracts

An abstract is a summary of a technical article that gives readers a condensed description of the topic and the key issues. Used with long or highly technical articles, abstracts can be part of the article or they can stand alone. In either case, they help readers determine whether they want to read the entire article, and they are useful for giving managers an overview of the topic. Abstracts also appear in journals such as *Biological Abstracts* with information on how to find the full-length article. The purpose of the abstract is to give the maximum amount of pertinent information in the minimum amount of space.

Abstracts differ from executive summaries because executive summaries include more detail and might even include charts and graphs. Also, executive summaries never stand alone; they are always part of a long report. The following are characteristics of abstracts:

- Abstracts are always short (200–250 words or less).
- They are written as a single paragraph, though it might be a very long paragraph.
- They are written for the same audience as the article, so they use the same level of technical language.
- They always summarize the main points of the results.
- They usually summarize the main points of the materials and methods, and of the discussion.

Specifications

A specification (or "spec") is a detailed statement of work. Specifications often describe materials, dimensions, and workmanship for building, installation, or manufacturing projects. Because unclear specifications can be costly in terms of delays and potential lawsuits, it is crucial that specifications be:

- Carefully researched
- Accurately written
- Carefully revised

The government requires agencies to write specifications when contracting for equipment or services. The specifications define exactly what the contractor is to provide: a technical description of the device; estimated cost; estimated delivery date; and standards for design, manufacture, workmanship, testing, training, governing codes, inspection, and delivery. Government specifications must comply with particular rules and formats, and government agencies publish guidelines on writing them.

Steps in developing specifications include:[8]

1. Get a statement of the problem and requirements.
2. Analyze and classify the problem and requirements.
3. Restate this requirements specification in your words to the contractor.
4. Begin your design specification process.

   When writing specifications:

   - Write clearly.
   - Use appropriate technical language.
   - Be precise.
   - Be concise.

- Be complete.

- Use the present tense—Not, "The equipment *will have* (or *must have* or *should have*) six components," but "The equipment *has* six components."

Online Help Systems

The purpose of online help is to give readers instant answers to their questions or problems and to put those answers where readers can find them easily. The first step in developing a help system is to examine the reader's needs. What will the reader want to know? What terms need to be defined? What questions might the reader ask? What procedures will the reader want to perform?

For an online help system, the technical writer develops a series of topics that explain common tasks and define terms. The writer then organizes these topics into many different types of devices, some of which are similar to those used in a printed document. Such devices include:

- *Table of contents*—a listing of all topics in the help system, divided into broad sections like the chapters in a book

- *Thematic index*—an index that lists all topics in the help text, with topics grouped by category (e.g., "drawing objects," "fields," "file formats")

- *Glossary*—a list of terms that might be unfamiliar to readers
- *Alphabetical index*—an index that lists all topics in the help text, sorted alphabetically by topic title or keyword
- *"How do I?" index*—an index of common tasks that users might perform

The difference between these online devices and their printed counterparts is the way the reader accesses the information. Instead of turning to a page, the reader might click on a hypertext link that jumps to and opens the online page that discusses the topic.

Online help systems also allow including other devices:

- *Pop-up boxes*—boxes that pop up on the screen when the user clicks on or places the cursor above specified words or phrases. (Such boxes are often used for quick explanations or short definitions of terms.)
- *Tutorials*—step-by-step programs that let readers learn at their own pace, receive feedback, and practice tasks.

- *Wizards*—software programs similar to tutorials that let the reader select the tasks instead of being directed along a predetermined path.

- *Coaches, agents, or assistants*—features that answer questions and also provide help topics and tips on tasks as the reader performs work. The reader can turn them on or off. Microsoft's animated paper clip is an example of an assistant.

- *"Show me" links*—hypertext links that, when clicked on, demonstrate the action the reader wants to perform.

- *Hypertext links*—links that, when clicked on, take the reader to a related topic or even to an outside source of more information, such as a website.

Tools for Creating Help Files

The most important tool for creating help files is the technical writer. The writer is responsible for developing a help system that meets the audience's needs. That requires:

- Careful audience analysis

- Clear writing

- Logical organization

- Bulleted and numbered lists whenever possible
- Thoughtful attention to such details as topic headings
- Short paragraphs and sentences
- Hyperlinks for cross-reference and additional information

For example, the most sophisticated help system in the world will not help if the topic discusses "landscape printing" and the reader only wants to "print the document on the wide part of the paper."

Because standard HTML documents are text-based, they can be created with any word-processing program. However, the codes and controls used to create help tables of contents and indexes are more complicated. To help with the "grunt work" of formatting and coding text, a number of software programs are available. Many software programs also allow single-source editing (creating one master Help file that can then be converted to different formats such as print or HTML).

Employers often expect technical writers to be familiar with these programs. Many of the programs are available free, if only on a trial basis, and many can be downloaded or ordered from the Internet. Some common authoring tools can be obtained as follows:

Program	Company Website
RoboHelp	www.adobe.com
HelpBreeze	www.solutionsoft.com
Microsoft HTML Help	www.microsoft.com

Computer- and Web-Based Training

Computer-based training (CBT) is a term used to describe any computer-delivered training, including training provided by means of a CD-ROM or the World Wide Web. It is an interactive instructional experience between a computer and a learner in which the computer provides most of the stimulus and the learner responds. Although some people use the term CBT interchangeably with CAI, computer-aided instruction, CBT has a more complicated branching program than CAI.

Web-based instruction (WBI) is usually considered one method of CBT. It is delivered over public or private computer networks and displayed by a web browser. WBI is available in many formats, and several terms are linked to it, e.g., on-line courseware, distance education online. WBI is not downloaded CBT, but rather on-demand training stored in a server and accessed across a network. The training provider controls access to the training.

Training by CD-ROM versus the Web

There are several factors to consider in deciding whether to deliver training through a CD-ROM or over the web. Some people like the convenience of simply inserting a self-starting CD-ROM. The CD-ROM is also useful because it can be sold in a bookstore or electronically. In addition, it allows the developer to download graphics that would take users too long to download.

An advantage of web-based instruction is that the developer can update material and correct errors with no loss of inventory or distribution time. Because the updates are completely invisible to users, the users don't have to wait for delivery of a new CD-ROM. Furthermore, there are no shipping charges.

The CBT Development Process

The following are steps in the CBT development process, though *each step might be visited and revisited many times:*[9]

1. Envision the solution. Consider how to optimize learning, meet the users' expectations, meet the client's requirements, and stay within your own constraints. Think about the following:

    - Time and money available (plan on at least twice as much time as you think)

- Life expectancy of the document and maintenance needs
- Distribution channels
- Level of multimedia
- Level of interactivity
- Business goals and learning objectives
- Minimal computer arrangement for users
- Available authoring and multimedia tools

2. Plan learners' experience. For your learners to interact with the material in a meaningful way, determine the following:

   - How to support the purpose and appeal to learners through tone, graphics, color, and fonts
   - Beginning knowledge of learners
   - Learning goals for the project and objectives for the individual learner
   - Measurements the client will use to determine success
   - Size of the average learning module

- Whether learners should go through the modules in a predetermined sequence or access individual modules as needed

- How learners will navigate from one module to the next

3. Create a storyboard for one module. A *storyboard* is a sketch of each screen, showing all the elements, both text and graphics. It can be drawn by hand or by computer. If the modules are similar and you're developing them yourself, you might be able to get by with just one master storyboard. However, if there's a significant variation from one module to the next or if you delegate the development to someone else, you need to create a storyboard for each module.

4. Get feedback on the one module from a sampling of target users, and get buy-in from stakeholders.

5. Create a paper or computer-generated prototype of each section, representing the navigational elements.

6. Get feedback on the prototypes from target users and buy-in from stakeholders.

7. Document each important decision in case clients forget what they agreed to.

8. Design the navigation mechanisms, including buttons, menus, interactive images, and any bits of responsive interaction.

9. Create a sample module and field-test it with target users.

10. Develop all the modules.

11. Make sure your prototype works on the computer platforms of target users.

12. Test for quality assurance. Go through each screen and choose every menu item and every button to make sure each one does what it's supposed to do. To record an error, print the screen, circle the incorrect item, and note the problem.

Tips for Computer- and Web-Based Training[10]

- *Strive for stand-alone content, screen by screen.* Reading large amounts of screen text is difficult for some people, especially for those who wear bifocals. Minimize it where you can. Also avoid spreading text on a single concept or idea over several screens.
- *Design course navigation so that it is as intuitive as you can make it.* Each time learners must think about what they have to do next to move ahead in the course, their concentration is disrupted. Make navigation and the structure of the course as transparent as possible to the learner. For instance, cues like "click NEXT to continue" are great if you have a button labeled NEXT. That same cue is questionable if your "next" button has only a right-pointing arrow.

- *Where possible, avoid automatically timed screen changes, unless the changes are timed to follow an audio script.* Automatically timed screen changes can disrupt concentration. Don't do it. Give the learner control over screen changes and presentation rate.
- *Provide clues so that learners will have some idea of what will happen when they do something.* Explicit directions like "Click Next to continue to the section test" prepare the learner for what will happen next and also reduce learner anxiety.
- *Select screen and text colors for a reason, and use those colors consistently throughout the course.* Be sure to devote adequate attention to color choices when you design content for CBT or WBT.
- *When applicable, display the screen's relative location in the learning event so the learner has an idea of "how much more before I'm finished with this section."* Learners need some idea of how much time is required for any given module. Provide some guidance as to where they are within the learning event so they can decide, for example, whether to finish the current lesson or sign off and continue after lunch. This reduces stress (which is no friend of learning).
- *Provide a "resume" function so that learners can restart from where they were when they signed off.* When you have a restart built into learning events, learners do not need to start over if the learning event is interrupted. This prevents loss of time and helps maintain learner morale and learning level.
- *Don't let the aesthetics of screen design compete with the message of the learning event.* Don't let your enthusiasm for a pretty picture interfere with the instructional material. To create a pleasing design without too many bells and whistles, many teams hire a graphic artist who understands instructional design.
- *Be cautious of humor.* Be careful not to include material that could offend anyone, especially if it deals with race, gender, creed, color, or other sensitive issues. Also avoid sarcasm. Sometimes a comment

intended as humor can be interpreted as sarcasm, resulting in anger or stress. Don't let your course get between your learner and the content!

- *Provide easy access to a glossary throughout the learning event where applicable.* Your CBT learning event might introduce terms that are unfamiliar to all or part of your audience. In cases where it's reasonable to expect a term to be new to your entire audience, define and explain the term when you first use it. In cases where terms are new to only part of your audience, consider using a hyperlink that pops up a definition only when the term is clicked.

MAKING TECHNICAL MATERIAL ACCESSIBLE

Whatever you write should be available to anyone who needs it. You can create content to maximize the accessibility to people with disabilities. This is especially important with technical writing. Not only do people with various kinds of disabilities need information from your website, for example, but also people using various types of browsers.

The following are suggestions for maximizing accessibility and making documentation clearer and more useful for everyone:

- Provide clear, concise descriptions of the product or initial setup, including a section or card that gets the reader up and running with the basic features.

- Keep the number of steps in a procedure short and the steps simple. People with cognitive impairments have difficulty following multistep processes.

- Keep sentence structure simple, limiting each sentence to one clause where possible. Long, complicated sentences are difficult for those with language difficulties, those for whom English is a second language, and some who are hearing impaired.

- Provide descriptions that do not require pictures, or that include both pictures and writing. Using only graphics can cause problems when transcribing to other media.

- Avoid using directional terms (left, right, up, down) as the only clue to location. Persons with cognitive impairments might have difficulty interpreting them. Blind users who rely on screen readers might also have a problem. (A screen reader is a software program that reads the contents of the screen aloud to a user.)

- Emphasize key information and put it near the beginning of the text. Use bullets or headings for additional emphasis.

- Keep paragraphs and sections short.

- Break up long passages of text with subheadings.

- In product documentation, document all keyboard shortcuts. The best format is a two-column table in which the first column describes the user task and the second column describes the shortcut.

- Provide closed captions, transcripts, or descriptions of audio content for those who have hearing impairments.

Creating Accessible Graphics and Designs

In 1998, Congress amended the Rehabilitation Act to require federal agencies to make their electronic and information technology accessible to people with disabilities. Inaccessible technology interferes with an individual's ability to obtain and use information quickly and easily. Section 508 (29 U.S.C. 794d) was enacted to eliminate barriers in information technology, to make new opportunities available for people with disabilities, and to encourage development of technologies that will help achieve these goals.

To make graphics and design more accessible for everyone, including those with color blindness:[11]

- Do not use color-coding alone. Use additional cues, such as underlines or text annotations.

- Use patterns as well as colors for charts and graphs.

- Avoid hard-to-read color combinations, such as red and green or light green and white. People with color blindness might have difficulty seeing the difference.

You can take several steps to enhance the accessibility of web pages for people with visual impairments, especially those who use screen readers:[12]

- Always provide *alt text,* the descriptive text that appears as an alternative to a graphic or image on web pages.
- Provide text links in addition to image maps.
- Write text links that are meaningful but brief.
- Make link text distinct, using redundant visual cues such as color and underline, so color-blind readers can identify text.
- If you use tables or frames, provide alternate pages without them.

Technical writing involves writing, editing, or publishing information related to technology, medicine, engineering, science, or a similar field. It is distinguished from other types of writing by the role of the writer, purpose, writing style, and subject matter.

Technical writing should be targeted to the technical proficiency and understanding of the readers. If you have a mixed audience, include enough data to satisfy the technical readers, while adding explanations where needed to help lay readers. Technical documents should have a minimum of text, clear organization, and a design that allows skimming. You can use a variety of techniques to help readers interpret documents in light of their own knowledge and expectations.

Terminology is critical in technical documents. Technical definitions can be informal, formal, or extended. Technical writers also frequently must describe mechanisms. In doing so, they explain the purpose, describe the mechanism as a whole, and then explain each part. In giving technical instructions, or explaining a process, the writer uses clear, concise language and short, simple steps.

Some other forms of technical writing are technical manuals, technical journal articles, abstracts, specifications, help systems, computer-based training, and web-based instruction. Journal articles, abstracts, and specs are typically written for an audience with some knowledge of the subject matter. Technical manuals are written for both technical and nontechnical readers. Help systems, computer-based instruction, and web-based instruction are all intended for a general audience.

Technical writing—and all writing—should be accessible to everyone, including those with disabilities. You can make your writing accessible by following the principles of plain language, as well as specific accessibility guidelines.

NOTES

1 James H. Shelton, *Handbook for Technical Writing* (Lincolnwood, IL: NTC Publishing Group, 1994).
2 Carol M. Barnum and Saul Carliner, *Techniques for Technical Communicators* (New York: Macmillan Publishing Co., 1993).
3 Maryann V. Piotrowski, *Effective Business Writing: A Guide for Those Who Write on the Job* (New York: HarperCollins, 1996), 71.
4 Ibid., 71–72.
5 Microsoft Help and Support, "HOW TO: Print Envelopes or Labels form a List of Addresses in Word 2000," Microsoft Corporation. Online at http://www.support.microsoft.com (accessed January 2008).
6 Plain Language Action and Information Network, "Johnson Space Center Manual (example 2): National Aeronautical and Space Administration." Online at http://www.plainlanguage.gov (accessed January 2008).
7 Gary Blake and Robert W. Bly, *The Elements of Technical Writing* (New York: Macmillan, 1993).
8 Ibid.
9 Sheryl Lindsell-Roberts, *Technical Writing for Dummies* (Hoboken, NJ: Wiley Publishing, Inc., 2001), 183–185.
10 Pete Blair, "Technical Training Tips – Group 3 (20–30), Tips for Computer and Web Based Training." Online at http://www.peteblair.com/tips3.htm (accessed January 2008). Used with permission.
11 Microsoft Corporation, *Microsoft Manual of Style for Technical Publications*, 3rd ed. (Redmond, WA: Microsoft Press, 2004), 113–115.
12 Ibid.

CHAPTER 12

Other Forms of Workplace Writing

◆ Doing Whatever Is Needed ◆

Jennifer, Brian, Latisha, and Craig were a team of writers charged with developing a budget justification statement. Today was the first team meeting.

"I guess we'd better decide who does what," Craig said.

The group decided that Jennifer and Brian would draft the document, Craig would develop the graphics, and Latisha and Craig would both edit.

"Do we know what our main goal is?" Jennifer asked. "I know we're asking for increased funding for the state school breakfast program, but are we clear on what the increased funding will do for the state?"

"And specifically, how it will affect *people* in the state," added Latisha.

Brian spoke up: "You're right. We need to think that through. And we also need to consider our audience—the legislators."

"I guess we have a lot of work ahead," said Craig. "Let's get out our calendars and set some milestones."

Today's writers need to develop a wide array of skills. They must be able to work with others on a team, as well as compose and/or edit a variety of documents.

Employees at all levels are asked to help compose budget justification statements; make outlines for briefings; ghostwrite; and help write or revise policies, procedures, and regulations.

COLLABORATIVE WRITING

Most business writing is collaborative writing. You are team-writing any time more than one person must be involved before the document is final. Even if one person writes the first draft on her or his own, it might go through many technical experts, managers, editors, and people savvy about the politics of the issue before it is released. Anyone involved in the writing process must know how to work with others—how to plan, organize, and give and take suggestions.

Guidelines for Collaborative Writing

The following are some guidelines for collaborative writing:

- All members of the team should understand who will draft, who will edit, and who will sign off on which sections of the document. Roles, responsibilities, and deadlines should be clarified as early as possible. If team members can't agree on roles, the delegator might need to assign them.

- Both delegators and writers need to communicate expectations and feelings. Any problems or frustrations that arise should be discussed and worked out.

- Team members should be certain that they fully understand the purpose, audience, and subject of the document.

  Delegators, writers, and reviewers should coordinate their work. They should develop a production schedule or milestone chart, build in extra time to allow for the unexpected, and make sure the deadlines are realistic for everyone.

- If more than one person is doing the writing, the project should be broken into manageable chunks and sections assigned accordingly. One of the editor's jobs is to make sure the document sounds as if one person wrote it.

- When several team members are using the same software, they can save time by using software tools:
  - Use the "track changes" feature to strike through or add text in a contrasting color without destroying the original text.
  - Select a split screen to display the original and the edited version with the changes highlighted.
- Reviewers should make constructive comments. To make the project a learning experience, they should refrain from editing and ask questions instead: "Have you included enough details here?" or "Is this headline clear enough?"

How Groups Work

Small groups have lives and personalities of their own. Like individuals, they go through stages of development. Being aware of these stages can help you understand some of the frustrations you might face when you collaborate on a writing project. The most common model of group development was first developed in the mid-1960s by Bruce Tuckman and involves four stages—forming, storming, norming, and performing:[1]

- *Forming.* In this initial stage, a group of people assembles for a particular purpose, such as writing a proposal or a major report. At this point, they are still a collection of individuals who might or might not have worked together before. They might not even know one another.

- *Storming.* Each individual now attempts to fit into the group. Group members raise individual issues and concerns that must be addressed before the group can develop further.

- *Norming.* Now that individual issues are resolved, group members establish standards for the group's behavior and performance. They set goals and objectives, and they assign roles and tasks.

- *Performing.* The group now functions as a unit, and its members work together productively. The group can now perform the tasks assigned to it and achieve its mission.

A group may go in and out of these stages. Group members might begin to storm, for example, right after a period of productive performing.

GHOSTWRITING

You might be asked to write a letter for someone else's signature or prepare a report or speech for an upper-level manager. On the other hand, you might ask others to do the same for you. Understanding the realities of ghostwriting can help you and your partner complete the project successfully.

Delegating the Task

Delegating work just to get it off your desk can be self-defeating if you are disappointed in the results and end up completing the task yourself.

Make sure you delegate the writing task to someone who understands the situation well enough to take on the job, and then make sure that you work closely with the person, especially if he or she has little experience writing. Make sure you're clear about exactly what you want and that you communicate your expectations to the writer.

Don't expect the writer to duplicate your style, but instead add some of your own personal touches before signing off on the document.

Taking on the Task

If you are the one asked to write the letter, speech, or report, make sure you understand the task as thoroughly as possible. Ask questions, become informed, and consider this a learning opportunity. If the document is long, write one section and get feedback from the person who asked you to write before going on to the rest. You should expect changes, even though the draft represents your best effort.[2]

BUDGET JUSTIFICATIONS

Competition for government resources is intense and requires careful planning and writing of budget requests. Writing skill could be the competitive edge that makes your budget request succeed next year.

The primary purpose of a written budget is to give friendly legislators the ammunition they need to argue your case and to justify their votes to their constituency. If you're concerned with the federal budget or a state budget, you have to direct your justification to several different audiences:

- Office of Management and Budget (OMB) examiners (for a federal budget)
- Agency budget staff
- Legislators and legislative staffers
- Lobbyists

Federal employees should be familiar with OMB Circular A-11, which provides technical policy guidance regarding the format and content of budgets submitted to OMB. You can find this document, which is issued annually, on OMB's website (www.whitehouse.gov/OMB).

In addition to the guidance provided by OMB, each agency issues formal and informal guidance regarding the budget request within the agency. Anyone involved in writing budget requests should follow carefully the directions contained in agency call letters or other documents governing budget submissions.

Since 2005 federal agencies have been required to submit a performance budget. This means that they must show how funding will help the agency achieve short- and long-term goals in pursuit of its mission. They must link the mission, strategic goals, programs, and long-term and annual performance goals.

Effective budget justifications usually describe events that are intended to occur within a year or more. Their time frame is the end of the budget year (September 30) unless a different time frame is stated. The budget justification describes *intended* outcomes, not *hoped-for* outcomes. These outcomes are within the agency's jurisdiction, program authority, and power.

Before you write, make sure you have reviewed and analyzed the following information:

- Agency's mission, strategic goals, and annual performance goals
- Means and strategies for achieving those goals
- Description of agency, legislative authority, and appropriation language
- For each activity:
  - Statement of functions and purpose
  - Description of changes requested for the budget year as compared to the current year
  - Productivity increase and management improvements
  - Summary of budget approved by OMB or comparable state agency
  - Historical tables:
    - Program costs linked to appropriations
    - Employment by organization unit
    - Obligations or costs by object class
    - Summary of workload indicators

As you organize the justification information, make sure you include:

- Goals
- Objectives
- Workloads
- Accomplishments
- Beneficiaries served
- Funding needs

Effective budget justifications are:

- *Meaningful.* They describe significant outcomes that affect people, not agencies or things. If possible, they should relate to people of importance to the audience.
- *Measurable.* They quantify the impact of the intended program on the country. They state the unit of measurement precisely and use verifiable data.
- *Clear.* They use precise names, action verbs, and plain language.
- *Realistic.* They allow for aggressive, achievable goals.

- *Comprehensive.* They explain everything in the best possible light, address their own weakest points, and answer the toughest questions before the questions are asked.

The justification should show clearly the cause-and-effect relationship between the funding and the achievement of the outcome or objective.

For example, if the objective is a 20 percent decrease in the number of malnutrition cases, the justification will document the relationship between the level of poverty and the incidence of malnutrition. It will also describe how requested grant funds will be distributed among the states, local food banks, and nonprofit organizations that feed qualified low-income families.

The budget strategy merges the agency's strategic plan with its political plan. The *strategic plan* addresses the agency's mission, goals, results-oriented objectives, performance measures, and strategies. The *political plan* addresses reasons why members of Congress or the legislature will support the budget.

Using an example of funding for school breakfasts, Phillip Blackerby and Melissa Hield show an effective way to structure a budget justification request (Figure 12-1):[3]

Figure 12-1 ◆ Sample Budget Justification Request

Paragraph	Purpose	Example
First	• Puts the strongest possible statement in the lead • Invites the reader to read on • Describes the primary result of the request Supporting sentences explain consequences, especially to local constituents	"With full funding, 75,000 children will improve their grades by an average of 109% and increase school attendance by an average of 20%. In the long run, these children will be less likely to drop out of school, commit crimes, or depend on welfare. As a result, future human service programs at all levels of government will have lighter caseloads and smaller funding needs."
Second	• Develops logic between results described in first paragraph and agency's actions • Shows how agency's funding leads to achieving results	"Studies show that a good breakfast increases concentration, and free breakfasts at school give pupils an incentive to attend school. Increased concentration and attendance improve grades by an average of 10% for School Breakfast Program participants. The program distributes funds by formulae to state Boards of Education for school district grants in the 100 hungriest counties. District programs work with local food banks to serve nutritious breakfasts to qualified grade school children from low income families."
Third and subsequent	• Show how specific changes in the funding level affect program performance described in first two paragraphs. • Address funding levels by object class.	"Requested funding increases the number of children receiving school breakfasts by 9.5% and extends eligibility from 85 of the hungriest counties to 100. This increased performance includes an 8.1% increase in grants and a net 1.4% decrease in administrative overhead. . . ."

Paragraph	Purpose	Example
Last	• Summarizes • Reinforces and strengthens primary point in first paragraph • Leaves a final and lasting impression on the reader • Should be memorable	"A good day starts with a good breakfast: a good life starts with a good education. Simply feeding hungry children breakfast improves their school performance now and keeps them out of jail and off the welfare rolls later."

BRIEFINGS AND PRESENTATIONS

"Public speaking" may mean presenting your idea to a committee of four coworkers or delivering a presentation to a group of 250 people. In either case, careful preparation and planning are essential.

The outstanding speakers you have heard and envied might have made it look easy. However, their ability to present their ideas effectively took effort. They spent their fair share of time preparing before they got up in front of their audience to speak.

Steps in Preparing for a Briefing or a Presentation

1. Analyze audience, situation, and speaker.

2. Determine goal.

   a. Why are you addressing this audience?

   b. What specific action do you want to see happen as a result of this presentation?

   c. Three months from now, what do you want people to remember?

3. Determine sources of data.

4. Gather information.

5. Determine main points and supporting ideas.

6. Organize ideas.

7. Formulate introduction and conclusion.

8. Prepare notes for delivery.

9. Practice.

10. Anticipate types of questions and questioners you might encounter and plan how you will respond to them.

Make an Opening Statement

How you begin is important. Your introduction will add to your listeners' initial impression of you.

You should attempt to do at least two things in your beginning remarks:

- Try to capture your listeners' attention. Using a strong opening will catch their immediate interest.

- Give at least a general indication of the topic and the direction of your talk. Make sure that your opening statement is related to the subject, understandable, and believable.

Try to avoid such common openings for speeches as:

- "Today I'm going to talk about . . ."

- A joke

  - Humor is difficult for most people to use. The material has to be good, and the speaker has to have a good sense of timing. Most people fall flat on their faces with jokes.

  - Unless the joke relates to the topic of your speech, it does nothing to orient your listeners to your topic.

  - Humor can be used effectively, but be careful!

Some effective ways to begin a presentation are:

- Use a striking or memorable quotation.

- Ask a question. (You don't expect your listeners to give you a verbal response; you want them to answer to themselves.)

- Make a startling statement.
- Use a vivid illustration (verbal).
- Create suspense.
- Use a humorous story—if it relates to the topic of your speech.

Relate to Your Listeners Personally

After you have caught your listeners' attention with your opening statement, you must maintain that interest by demonstrating immediately how the subject affects them personally. Answer the question, "Why do I need to hear what you are telling me?"

Give Examples

Even after you have attracted their attention and aroused their personal interest in your idea, you still need to win over your listeners. They will most certainly want to be shown. The burden for proof is on you.

You must back up your statements with facts, proof, evidence, concrete examples, and quotes. Case histories or proven systems make for good listening or reading. Also use visual material; the bulk of our perceptions come through the sense of sight. Facts are invaluable tools in maintaining interest and overcoming skepticism. Make sure any facts and figures you give are correct.

Conclude

If the speech has been lengthy, it's a good idea to briefly restate the major points. This helps your listeners remember what you have said.

Finally, sound a strong call to action. You presented your major points for some particular reason. In any presentation, the conclusion must be strong and forceful. It must be planned to answer satisfactorily the audience's legitimate question: "So what?"

To maximize the final impact, you might try one of the following methods:

- Use a striking or memorable quotation.
- Ask a question. (You expect your listeners to respond to themselves, and you know what the response will be.)
- Make a startling statement.
- Give a vivid illustration.
- Tell a humorous story—if it relates.

- Issue a challenge or an appeal. (This is more useful for a persuasive speech than for an informative one.)

WRITING POLICIES

A *policy* is a statement of principles or guidelines that helps organizations to enforce rules consistently.

Why Written Policies Are Important

Carefully written employment policies provide the structure within which an organization governs its employee relations. Sound policies can serve as both an effective communication device and a legal protection. A policies and procedures manual lets managers and employees know what is expected and prevents misunderstandings. Also, supervisors and managers are more likely to apply policies consistently when the policies are clearly communicated in writing. Finally, well-written policies show commitment to a positive work environment and to fair employment practices.

How Policies Develop

Policies reflect the views of the organization as a whole in a given area. Their authority usually comes from prior consensus—formal or informal. The following are the most common ways in which policies are created or modified:

- Documenting a practice that is already in place or is simple enough that consensus can be easily reached. For example, an organization might formalize a policy regarding employee gift-giving that has already become established.

- Proposing a policy for review and consideration by the organization. This might follow a sudden change, such as the bombing of the World Trade Center, which led to the adoption of policies regarding security.

- Creating or modifying policy to clarify an area that is unclear or that has gradually become a problem. After employees gained access to the Internet in the 1990s, some employees began to spend too much time on non-work-related websites or on personal email. As a result, organizations began to write policies governing Internet access.

- Although written policies in general are not legally required, certain policies might be required, or at least needed, in helping to establish good-faith compliance with federal and state law. For example, the Supreme Court has indicated that employers may protect themselves against liability for sexual harassment by having clearly articulated policies against sexual harassment that include effective complaint procedures.

Guidelines for Writing Policies

- Avoid imposing policies from the top down. Try to work with what is already good practice within your organization or work group.
- Consult widely. Talk to people within your organization. Make a special effort to engage potential critics of the new policy. Also, see what policies are working well for other organizations and adopt them for your own if they fit.
- Keep policies general so that they can be implemented easily. Avoid precise rules that try to cover every situation that might arise. Try to avoid all-inclusive lists such as work rules.
- Steer clear of any promises that could be interpreted as a contract. For example, don't state that the organization will "only" or "always" do something or "must" act in a particular way.
- Give appropriate examples to illustrate your policies. A well-chosen example can often make things far clearer than long, detailed descriptions can.
- Provide plenty of time for discussion. Allow people time to think about the new guidelines. Avoid letting them feel that you are pushing through new policy to avoid discussion.

Components of the Policy

To write the policy, include the following information. The examples given come from "Recommended Executive Branch Model Policy/Guidance on 'Limited Personal Use' of Government Office Equipment Including Information Technology," issued by the Chief Information Office Council of the General Services Administration:[4]

- State your purpose. "This document provides general recommended policy, or a model, for assisting agencies or departments in defining acceptable use conditions for Executive Branch employee personal use of Government office equipment including information technology."
- Give any background (general principles, etc.) needed to further clarify the purpose of the policy. "Taxpayers have the right to depend on their Government to manage their tax dollars wisely and effectively. . . . Executive Branch employees should be provided with a professional supportive work environment. They should be given the tools needed to effectively carry out their assigned responsibilities."
- Identify the authority for the policy. "Authority for this policy is cited as 5 U.S.C. sec 301 which provides that the head of an executive department or military department may prescribe regulations for the use

of its property; and Executive Order 13011, Federal Information Technology, section 3(a)(1), which delineates the responsibilities of the Chief Information Office (CIO) Council in providing recommendations to agency heads relating to the management and use of information technology resources."

- Identify to whom the policy applies. "Agency officials may apply this policy to contractor personnel, interns, and other non-government employees through incorporation by reference in contracts or memorandums of agreement as conditions for using Government office equipment and space."

- Give the date when the policy goes into effect. "This model makes use of material already implemented in various agencies or departments' personal use policies and can be implemented [immediately] unless superseded by any other applicable law or regulation. . . ."

- Provide any definitions needed to clarify the policy. "Personal use means any activity that is conducted for purposes other than accomplishing official or otherwise authorized activity."

- Establish the standards for the policy. (Remember, standards should be measurable in terms of quality, quantity, or time.) "Misuse or inappropriate personal use of government equipment includes . . . the creation, copying, transmission, or retransmission of chain letters or other unauthorized mass mailings regardless of subject matter."

The following is part of a sample telework policy and agreement issued by the Office of Personnel Management to federal agencies.

Sample Telework Policy and Agreement[5]

United States Office of Personnel Management
"Balancing Work and Family Demands Through Telecommuting"

Sample Agreement

Between Agency and Employee Approved for Telecommuting on a Continuing Basis

The supervisor and the employee should each keep a copy of the agreement for reference.

Voluntary Participation

Employee voluntarily agrees to work at the agency-approved alternative workplace indicated below and to follow all applicable policies and procedures. Employee recognizes that the telecommuting arrangement is not an employee benefit, but an additional method the agency may approve to accomplish work.

Trial Period

Employee and agency agree to try out the arrangement for at least [specify number] months unless unforeseeable difficulties require earlier cancellation.

Salary and Benefits

Agency agrees that a telecommuting arrangement is not a basis for changing the employee's salary or benefits

Duty Station and Alternative Workplace

Agency and employee agree that the employee's official duty station is [indicate duty station for regular office] and that the employee's approved alternative workplace is: [specify street and number, city, and state].

Note: All pay, leave, and travel entitlements are based on official duty station.

Official Duties

Unless otherwise instructed, employee agrees to perform official duties only at the regular office or agency-approved alternative workplace. Employee agrees not to conduct personal business while in official duty status at the alternative workplace, for example, caring for dependents or making home repairs.

Work Schedule and Tour of Duty

Agency and employees agree that employee's official tour of duty will be: [specify days, hours, and location, i.e., the regular office or the alternative workplace].

Time and Attendance

Agency agrees to make sure the telecommuting employee's timekeeper has a copy of the employee's work schedule. The supervisor agrees to certify biweekly the time and attendance for hours worked at the regular office and the alternative workplace. (Note: Agency may require employee to complete self-certification form.)

Leave

Employee agrees to follow established office procedures for requesting and obtaining approval of leave.

> **Overtime**
> Employee agrees to work overtime only when ordered and approved by the supervisor in advance and understands that working overtime without such approval may result in termination of the telecommuting privilege and/or other appropriate action.

DRAFTING REGULATIONS

A regulation is an official rule, law, or order stating what may or may not be done or how something must be done; an order issued by a government department or agency that has the force of law. As noted earlier, government agencies at all levels—federal, state, and local—are working to word regulations in plain language. The Office of the Federal Register, National Archives and Records Administration, provides a guide to legal writing at www.archives.gov/federal-register/write/legal-docs.[6]

The topics the guide covers include:

- Arrangement
- Headings
- Purpose clause
- Definitions
- Ambiguity

- Principles of clear writing
- Cross-references
- Punctuation, capitalization, typography, and spelling
- Format requirements for regulatory documents
- Words and expressions to avoid
- Preferred expressions

To show how plain language can improve legal writing, Joseph Kimble gives the following example of a before-and-after provision:[7]

Example 1: Consultant Contract

Before

The CONSULTANT agrees to fully complete the described assignment and furnish same to the DEPARTMENT by __________ calendar days after notification of Approval, it being fully understood and agreed by the parties hereto that in the event the CONSULTANT shall fail to do so as aforesaid, the DEPARTMENT shall, without the necessity of notice, terminate the services of said CONSULTANT without incurring any liability for payment for services submitted after said due date or shall deduct, as a liquidation of damages, a sum of money equal to one-third of one percent (1/3 of 1%) per calendar day of the total fee if the performance of the entire contract is delayed beyond the due date. Upon written request by the CONSULTANT an extension of time may be granted by the DEPARTMENT in writing, in the event the CONSULTANT has not received from the DEPARTMENT proper information needed to complete the assignment or, in the event other extenuating circumstances occur, the time may be similarly extended. It is further agreed that if a liquidation of damages is imposed pursuant to the aforesaid provisions, any money due and payable to the DEPARTMENT thereby may be retained out of any money earned by the CONSULTANT under the terms of this contract.

After

The Due Date for the Work

The Consultant must complete and deliver the work by _______ calendar days after receiving notice that the Department has approved this contract. The Consultant may ask in writing for more time, and the Department may grant it in writing, if

(a) the Consultant does not receive from the Department the information needed to complete the work; or

(b) there are other extenuating circumstances.

If the Consultant Misses the Due Date

If the Consultant fails to deliver the work by the due date, the Department may—without having to give notice—choose either one of the following:

(a) terminate the Consultant's services, and not pay for services that are submitted after the due date; or

(b) claim liquidated damages of 1/3 of 1% of the total contract payment for each calendar day late, and subtract this amount from the total payment.

Jim Harte and Umeki Thorne, both program analysts at the General Services Administration, clarified and streamlined a 194-word rule on government-sponsored travel down to 45 words.[8]

Example 2: Federal Travel Regulation

Before

Section 301-2.5(b) Indirect-route or interrupted travel.

When a person for his/her own convenience travels by an indirect route or interrupts travel by a direct route, the extra expenses shall be borne by him/her. Reimbursement for expenses shall be based only on such charges as would have been incurred by a usually traveled route. An employee may not use contract airline/rail passenger service provided under contract with the General Services Administration (see part 301-15, subpart B, of this chapter) for that portion of travel by an indirect route which is for personal convenience. Additionally, an employee may not use a U.S. Government Transportation Request (GTR) (see section 301-10.2 of this chapter) or a contractor-issued charge card (see part 301-15, subpart C, of this chapter) for procurement of commercial carrier transportation services for that portion of travel by an indirect route which is for personal convenience. An employee may, however, use contract airline/rail passenger service, as well as a GTR or contractor-issued charge card, for portions of travel that are authorized to be performed at Government expense. (See section 301-11.5(a) of this chapter regarding reimbursement claims for travel that involves an indirect route.)

After

Section 301.10.8. What is my liability if, for personal convenience, I travel or use an indirect route?

If you travel on government business by anything other than the most direct, least-cost route available, you must pay for the added costs so the taxpayers don't.

INTEROFFICE MEMOS

An interoffice memo is a written record or communication within a business setting. Many organizations provide computerized or printed forms to standardize and simplify the treatment of key information. This information includes the name of the recipient, the names of anyone who is receiving a copy, the sender, the date, and the subject or reference. Memos can be as short as one page or as long as three pages—and occasionally longer. Whenever possible, these messages should be limited to one page and should contain only succinct, need-to-know information.

Memos are especially useful for recording an agreement, transmitting information, making a case, requesting data, and enabling action.

Steps in Writing a Memo

Identify your purpose, audience, and topic. Think about what your readers need to know and how best to present the information to them.

Organize your thoughts, using a Mind Map and outline if needed. Make sure your information is accurate, relevant, and unbiased (unless you're designated as an advocate). Present the bad news as well as the good so that your readers can make the right decisions.

Use your organization's memo template or create your own format, including the key elements. One way to format a memo is shown below.[9]

MEMORANDUM

DATE:

TO:

FROM:

RE:

CC:

Once you've created your draft, review your memo for correctness, clarity, and conciseness. Make sure that you placed the main point or purpose early in the message and that you spelled out specifically what actions the reader needs to take.

Because of changes in the methods and variety of workplace writing, writers, editors, and reviewers need flexibility and team-building skills. Collaborative team-writing occurs whenever two or more people are involved in writing or approving a document. Teams are more productive when they communicate clearly, coordinate their work, and understand the stages of group development.

Clear communication is also essential in the ghostwriting process. Understanding the realities of ghostwriting can help you and your partner complete the project successfully.

The budget justification describes intended outcomes that are within the agency's jurisdiction, program authority, and power. The primary purpose of a written budget is to provide friendly legislators the ammunition they need to argue your case and to justify their votes to their constituency. Effective justification statements are meaningful, measurable, clear, realistic, and comprehensive.

Whether you give a briefing to a group of four or a presentation to a packed auditorium, thorough preparation and planning are essential. Effective beginnings and conclusions especially require careful thought.

Writing policies and regulations requires absolute clarity and logical organization. A policy is statement of principles or guidelines that provides a basis for consistent rule-making and resource allocation. A regulation, on the other hand, is an order issued by a government department or agency that has the force of law. While policies are general, regulations are specific. Policies, regulations, and other types of legal writing benefit from the application of plain language. Both the Plain Language Action and Information Network and the National Archives provide specific guidance for writing regulations, as well as for writing other types of government documents.

Interoffice memos are especially useful for recording an agreement, transmitting information, making a case, requesting data, and enabling action. Many organizations have their own forms or templates for memos. Like emails, memos should be clear and concise and should be limited to one page whenever possible.

NOTES

1 Resources describing Tuckman's model of group development abound. See for example: Helena Smalman Smith, "Forming, Storming, Norming, Performing: Helping new teams perform effectively, quickly," Mind Tools Ltd. Online at http://www.mindtools.com/pages/article/newLDR_86.htm (accessed January 2008).

2 Maryann V. Piotrowski, *Effective Business Writing: A Guide for Those Who Write on the Job* (New York: HarperCollins, 1996), 61–62.

3 Phillip Blackerby and Melissa Hield, "Tips on Writing Effective Budget Justifications," *Armed Forces Comptroller* (Spring 1988). Used with permission.

4 Chief Information Office Council of the General Services Administration, "Recommended Executive Branch Model Policy/Guidance on 'Limited Personal Use' of Government Office Equipment Including Information Technology." Online at www.govexec.com (accessed November 2007).

5 United States Office of Personnel Management, "Balancing Work and Family Demands Through Telecommuting." Online at http://www.mwcog.org/commuter/fedpolicy.html (accessed January 2008).
6 The Office of the Federal Register, National Archives and Records Administration, "Drafting Legal Documents." Online at http://www.archives.gov/federal-register/write/legal-docs (accessed March 2008).
7 Joseph Kimble, "Answering the Critics of Plain Language," *The Scribes Journal of Legal Writing* (1994–1995). Online at http://www.plainlanguagenetwork.org/kimble/critics.htm (accessed January 2008).
8 Plain Language Action and Information Network, "Legal Examples: GSA Travel Regulations." Online at http://www.plainlanguage.gov (accessed January 2008).
9 For detailed information on how to format a memorandum, see William A. Sabin's *The Gregg Reference Manual,* 10th ed. (New York: McGraw-Hill, 2005), Section 13.

APPENDIX

Exercise Answers

CHAPTER 2

Test Yourself: Who Is the Audience?

1. Audience: Electronics engineers at radar-equipped airfields. These readers are assumed to have highly technical knowledge of the topic.

2. Audience: Airport manager. This reader has a general but not highly technical understanding of the topic.

3. Audience: Chamber of Commerce members. This audience is assumed to have the least knowledge of the topic. This version is most easily understood and appeals to the general reader.

Test Yourself: Selecting the Purpose and Sequence

Read the following paragraphs. Select the paragraph that states the purpose. Put a "1" next to it. Then use the numbers 2, 3, 4, and 5 to indicate the appropriate sequence for the remaining paragraphs.

1. We are happy to announce that our new headquarters are ready for occupancy. We have scheduled the move for September 25. Before then, however, we would like each of you to visit the new offices.

2. The address of the building is 700 Market Street, which is between Maple Avenue and Grant Street. The building is a large, 10-story brick building set back from the street.

3. We will occupy the entire eighth and ninth floors. To reach the reception area, take the lobby elevator and go to the eighth floor. When you get there, someone will show you to your office. Most of the sales offices will be on the eighth floor, while other offices, including research and development, as well as finance and administration, will be on the ninth floor.

4. Most of the offices will have the new desks, chairs, and bookcases that you selected. Some offices will include additional chairs and tables.

5. Please check your office and make sure everything you ordered is there. We look forward to hearing from you and hope you will let us know of anything you need.

Question: What ordering system would you use to organize these paragraphs?

Answer: Order of location (spatial or geographic order)

CHAPTER 3

Test Yourself: Organizing Paragraphs

A. Putting the Main Idea Up Front and Cutting Ideas that Don't Belong

Read over the seven sentences that follow. Then decide how you would make a unified, well-planned paragraph out of them.

The entire lab procedure went as planned. The only problem was minor, and it occurred when we removed one of the samples from its shipping container. As we took the bag from the shipping container, the bag broke open. The sample shattered when it fell onto the table. Fortunately, we had an extra sample from that same location.

B. Making New Paragraphs

Expressed in a single paragraph, the material that follows looks massive and uninviting. How would you break it up into five paragraphs? Indicate where you would make paragraph breaks by inserting paragraph symbols (¶).

The term "white paper" originated in the early 20th century in England. This type of writing was used to differentiate short government position papers from longer, more detailed reports. The shorter position papers were bound in white covers, while the longer reports were bound in blue covers. Today's white papers are rarely bound and have evolved into more versatile documents.

So what exactly is a white paper in today's business world? Although there is not an exhaustive definition covering the wide range of papers called white papers, the most comprehensive definition is "a communication tool used to explain something complex to an audience with little to no background on the topic." Research shows that people use white papers as means of first learning about a given topic or product.

A common thread among white papers is the use of a problem and solution. Rather than beginning by just naming the merits of a product or service like a marketing brochure, the white paper usually highlights a problem that is common with the target audience. After clearly outlining a problem, a good white paper shows how the reader can use the product or service to solve the problem.

White papers work well as a marketing tool for many reasons. Besides being very industry-specific and consumer-focused, white papers make great justifications for customers wanting to purchase the service or product. There is no better way for employees to explain the need for a product or service to their bosses than presenting a well-written document by an industry expert clearly outlining the problems and the benefits. It grabs attention initially and has a strong pull all the way to the point of sale.

The single industry where white papers proliferate is information technology. The industry changes so fast that IT professionals are constantly facing new problems and solutions. White papers play a vital role in this industry by helping both marketers and customers. Most IT websites have hundreds of white papers available for download, and the best part is that they are almost always free.

Test Yourself: Writing Topic Sentences

Add a topic sentence to the beginning of each of the following paragraphs. The following are some examples:

1. Writers should consider three characteristics of their readers when planning a document.

---

2. We selected Barbara, John, and Cheryl for the ABC Project.

Test Yourself: Overloaded Sentences

Rewrite the following sentence to make it clearer. The following is an example revision:

The National Transportation Safety Board today announced that it has completed an investigation of the midair collision of a commercial plane and a twin-engine private plane, which resulted in the deaths of 34 people. The investigation showed that, immediately before impact, the private plane had made a 360-degree roll. The report stated that both planes had been in an air corridor that was restricted to oncoming commercial flights. The board concluded that, in all probability, the accident was the result of pilot error.

Test Yourself: Sound Sentences

A. Classifying Sentences

Some of the following sentences are complete. Others are run-on sentences, while others are sentence fragments. In front of the number for each sentence, put the symbol that applies:

C *for complete sentence*
R *for run-on sentence*
F *for sentence fragment*

1. F
2. R
3. C
4. C
5. F
6. C
7. C
8. F
9. C
10. F

B. Complete the Sentence

Make complete sentences out of these fragments:

1. Sir Alexander Fleming is an immunologist, whose reputation as the discoverer of penicillin almost rivals that of Jonas Salk, who invented the polio vaccine.

2. Sue cooked dinner while Rudy cleaned the house.

3. Although the case had been closed for 17 years, the investigators found new evidence.

4. Sam is a good friend whose advice I have valued over the years.

5. The auto mechanic assured us the repairs would be minor. He then proceeded to list a dozen things wrong with the car.

6. The employees, finding that they could no longer work under such stressful conditions and with so few benefits, quit their jobs.

7. Police chiefs want to hire more officers, but not without additional funds.

C. Using Punctuation in Sentences

Insert or substitute proper punctuation to remedy these run-on sentences:

1. On the one hand, he is a careful worker; on the other hand, he takes too long to complete his assignments.

2. You can count on Mark to help you out; he's very reliable.

3. There are two reasons why you should take that trip to Atlanta: one is to meet with the regional director, and the other is to check on our suppliers.

Test Yourself: Rewriting Tom's Letter

Reread the vignette at the beginning of this chapter. Take the suggestions given by Brad and rewrite Tom's paragraph. The following is a suggested revision.

Honesty is the hallmark of Marcia's character. Her honesty extends from areas where we easily see it (in relationships and business transactions) to integrity of thought. Scientific, thorough, and meticulous, she approaches any analytical task with an exacting eye. This is what I mean by integrity of thought.

I have always been impressed by Marcia's helpfulness and willingness to help others, regardless of their position. She also is pleasant to work with, and she takes the time to help those who are learning their way. For example, last week she stayed late to help a coworker complete a task that was behind schedule.

CHAPTER 4

Test Yourself: Changing Passive Voice to Active Voice

Rewrite the following sentences. Change passive voice to active voice. Say things as directly as you can. Supply the subject of the sentence when necessary. The following are suggested answers.

1. The managers chose Leslie Brooks employee of the year.
2. The police gave us an escorted tour of the jail.
3. Did the reviewers recommend that film?
4. The software company gave our agency a presentation.
5. The guest speaker explained how to sell a product.
6. The accounting department distributed an incorrect version of the policy.
7. It became clear that the witnesses misrepresented the facts.
8. The police recommend that you stick to the main roads.

9. Did the company rehire him?

10. We appreciate your help.

11. The job requires a college degree and five years of experience.

12. The investigating committee determined that the nomination should be withdrawn.

Test Yourself: Bringing Submerged Verbs to the Surface

Rewrite the following sentences. Change passive voice to active voice. Bring the submerged verbs to the surface. Say things as directly as you can. You'll find you can eliminate many words in the process. The following are suggested answers.

1. These reports concern the development of new safety measures.

2. He proposed a solution to the problem.

3. Mr. Huffman paid today.

4. The employees recognized I-Hsin for her persistence and hard work.

5. We are finally progressing toward our major goals.

6. The legislative subcommittee determined yesterday that our agency would continue to receive funding.

7. The auditors checked all expenditures from the past quarter.

8. Janet and Malik analyzed that report.

9. We recommend that the agency distribute nonperishable foods to the homeless.

10. After carefully reviewing the evidence, the jury decided to acquit the man.

11. These changes will streamline our process.

12. The contract was finalized yesterday. *(For active voice: The agency finalized the contract yesterday.)*

Test Yourself: Improving Your Tone

Rewrite these lines to give them a friendlier, more confident tone. The following are suggested answers.

1. The proposed high-speed boats will have ample speed for at least 85 percent of suspect chases.

2. The regulatory program will protect the public from companies that place profits ahead of service to consumers.

3. Please feel free to call if you have any questions. I'm available from 9 a.m. to 5 p.m. on weekdays.

4. Please sign the application so we can proceed.

5. Please note our new time-keeping policy.

6. This software program helps accountants complete their tasks on time. Our beta testing indicates that monthly reports were out on time or within a few days of the deadline. This is an improvement over what we saw in the past.

7. Please review these steps in the manual and be sure to follow them.

8. We received your request for the balance of your benefit check. You should receive it by the beginning of next week.

9. Kate took the visitors to the customer service office.

10. Please review the enclosed personnel handbook and sign off or note any desired changes by February 20.

CHAPTER 5

Test Yourself: Finding a Better Way to Say It

Translate each of the following gobbledygook statements into relaxed, straightforward business English. The following are suggested answers.

1. Because of some security problems this past year, we have new procedures for visitor tours.

2. Search all visitors and remove any questionable items from their briefcases or handbags.

3. Distribute badges to all visitors, and then take them first to the courthouse.

4. In accordance with agency regulations, do not allow visitors near any sensitive material.

5. If a visitor wanders into unauthorized areas or looks at sensitive material, gather all visitors and take them out of the building.

6. We ask your cooperation in following these regulations to help ensure our security.

Test Yourself: Deflating Words

Replace each inflated word with a short word (or with two or three short words). The following are suggested answers (in the right-hand column).

1. communicate	1. tell
2. component	2. part
3. constitute	3. make up
4. necessitate	4. need, require
5. depart	5. leave
6. magnitude	6. size
7. convene	7. meet
8. exhibit (verb)	8. show
9. equitable	9. fair, just, impartial
10. transmit	10. send

Test Yourself: Deflating Sentences

To deflate these sentences, you'll have to interpret them. Rewrite each sentence to clarify its meaning; express the thought in an entirely different way if you like. Cut any unnecessary words. Whenever you can replace long words with short ones, or unfamiliar words with familiar ones, do so. The following are suggested answers.

1. You will move ahead faster and make more money as you make the best use of your abilities.

2. We believe your plan for reducing injuries will not work.

3. The current procedure does not make the best use of our personnel.

4. Radioactivity is currently a possibility. [*When is radioactivity* not *excessively dangerous? Note also that "presently" can mean either "right now" or "soon." Use another, more specific word.*]

5. Most students were not well prepared, and they made many mistakes.

Test Yourself: Avoiding Repetition

Read the two examples of repetitious sentences below. Write a shorter, clearer version of each sentence. The following are suggested answers.

– You may request an appeal, and you may also request a personal appearance before the appeals board.

– If you make a hole while freeing a stuck vehicle, you must fill the hole before you drive away.

Test Yourself: Making the Parts Parallel

The following are suggested answers.

A. *The following is a list of requirements for a college instructor. Make the parts of this outline match.*

1. Quality of classroom teaching

    a. Knowledge of the subject

    b. Ability to relate to students

    c. Responsiveness to questions

2. Contributions to the university

3. Contributions to the community

    a. Volunteer work related to instructor's field of expertise

    b. Volunteer work outside the instructor's field

4. Quality and quantity of instructor's publications

B. *Here is part of an outline for a presentation on the qualities of a successful manager. Tighten it by making the parts match.*

- Can cope with stressful situations
- Is a good role model
- Knows how to foster teamwork
- Communicates clearly at all levels
- Takes responsibility

C. *Rewrite the following sentences to make the parts match.*

1. The history course was stimulating and challenging.
2. If you want to buy shares in Fund XYZ by mail, fill out and sign the account application form, make your check payable to "The XYZ Fund," and write your Social Security number on your check.
3. She signed up for courses in cake decorating and watercolor design.

4. My favorite sports are golf in the fall, tennis in the spring, and skiing in the winter.

5. He couldn't decide whether to take the job or go to graduate school as he had planned.

Test Yourself: Painting a Clear Picture

Read the following statements. Now read into them. Use your imagination. Replace each statement with one that is specific. Make it interesting and informative. Write more than one sentence if you like. The following are suggested answers.

1. The report related to the city's annual budget and how it affects employee benefits.

2. Yesterday we had two inches of rain and winds up to 40 miles an hour.

3. You must check the system at least once a month.

4. She spent two months working on the presentation.

5. The boss likes your idea so well that he is going to recommend it to upper management.

6. I plan to apply for a job in the private sector within the next month.

CHAPTER 7

Test Yourself: Line Editing a Letter

Suppose the letter below were going out over your signature. What changes would you make before mailing it? Examine the letter for things that look or sound strange. Look out for inconsistencies, omissions, errors, problems with tone and style, submerged verbs, and parts that aren't parallel. Is the letter understandable? Is the phrasing precise? Circle each mistake you notice and rewrite the letter.

Dear Mrs. Phillips:

The following is a summary of changes planned for this year's Youth Leadership Institute (YLI) program.

Screening of Instructors

More than 70% of our participants said that last year's YLI program was the best leadership-training program in the state. However, the program showed the need to provide 24-hour monitoring of program participants. Therefore, the Behavioral Sciences Department suggested that this year's instructors undergo new screening procedures. This screening would identify whether instructors have:

- a background in psychology (needed to provide 24-hour monitoring of students);
- crisis counseling abilities; and
- no substance abuse problems.

We are preparing to begin the screening this year, with help from the Behavioral Sciences and Personnel departments.

Improved Survey

We have found that we need a better way to measure our participants' progress during the program. Each year we ask students to evaluate their progress at the YLI program. Unfortunately, students last year seemed unwilling to discuss their concerns, so the evaluation did not reflect their progress accurately.

Therefore, we are developing a new survey that uses both instructor-led interviews and anonymous questionnaires. Both surveys will be administered every two weeks. Students will participate in both programs, and instructors will use the anonymous questionnaire results to gauge the overall progress of the students. We hope to have more accurate results with this new system.

Thank you for your interest in the YLI program. We will send you copies of all pertinent forms and questionnaires when they become available. Please call if you need more information.

Sincerely,

YLI Program Director

CHAPTER 8

Test Yourself: Stating the Subject and Purpose

Give each email a more informative subject statement. Then write a one- or two-sentence opening that makes the purpose clear. The following are examples.

SUBJECT: Procedures for Internal Meetings Adopted

Attached are the newly adopted internal meeting procedures developed by Bill.

SUBJECT: Updated Audiovisual Form Attached

The trainers have approved the audiovisual form with slight changes.

Test Yourself: Rewriting an Email

Read over the email below and rewrite it. Delete all unnecessary and inappropriate information. Then organize the remaining data into a succinct, readable message. The following is a suggested answer.

SUBJECT: Request for Writing Course

We'd like you to organize a business-writing course for the division. Here are the specifics:

- June or July 2008
- Two or three days in duration
- 15 participants, including program analysts, budget analysts, engineers, and managers
- Conference room on third or fifth floor
- Instructor with federal service experience

I appreciate your help with this. Please let me know if you have any questions.

CHAPTER 9

Test Yourself: Rewriting a Letter

Rewrite the following letter using any of the techniques discussed in this chapter—indented lists, headings, question-and-answer formats, and if-then tables—that seem appropriate. The following is an example revision.

To: All School Bus Drivers
Re: Limiting Bus Idling

The State School Transportation Association has teamed up with the State Environmental Agency and the Greentown School District to protect schoolchildren and each of you from excessive exposure to diesel exhaust emissions. As part of this effort, we support and encourage you to follow their guidelines restricting engine idling time whenever practical, effective immediately.

Guidelines for Limiting Bus Idling

To the extent possible, eliminate idling by taking the following steps:

1. Shut off all engines while waiting for passengers to board at place of origin.
2. Shut off all engines as soon as practical after arriving at your location.
3. Follow the guidelines for maximum engine idling, according to the following table:

If the temperature is	*Then the maximum idling time is*
above 32° F	3 minutes
between −10° and 32° F	10 minutes
Below −10° F	Unlimited

Benefits of Following Guidelines

Please help us do our part to reduce air pollution and protect children's (and your own) health. Minimizing vehicle idling will also save money by reducing fuel consumption and engine wear.

Thank you for your support and cooperation with this effort.
Greentown School Bus Drivers Doing Their Share for Clean Air!

Sincerely yours,

Fleet Manager

CHAPTER 10

Test Yourself: The Report's Tone

Rewrite the following report to give it a more personal tone and make it more interesting to read. The following is an example revision.

Bennett County Hospital
Preliminary Report 2
June 16, 20xx

Submitted to the Board of Trustees
by the Review Committee

We are pleased to submit the second of three reports that you requested for your study of the feasibility of expanding Bennett County Hospital. We will submit the third report within three months and will include the data that you requested in your December 2, 2006, letter.

General Information

For the first time, Bennett County Hospital has received full accreditation from the highest national authority on hospital accreditation, the Joint Commission on Accreditation of Hospitals.

The hospital received this full accreditation because its personnel, services, and physical plant meet or exceed high professional standards.

In the past year, the hospital took the following steps to enhance the quality of service provided:

- Upgraded intensive care facilities
- Made a comparative study of nurses' salaries
- Increased nurses' salaries to maintain a well-qualified staff
- Began holding monthly meetings to maintain the cooperation of staff, administration, and trustees ...

CHAPTER 11

Test Yourself: Writing a Mechanism Description

Using the guidelines above, write a description of a computer mouse. The following is an example description.

A computer mouse is a device that controls the movement of the cursor or pointer on a display screen. A *mechanical* mouse is a small object that can be rolled along a hard, flat surface. Its name is derived from the shape of its early model, which looked a bit like a mouse. It is designed to fit into an adult's hand. It has a rubber or metal ball on its underside that can roll in all directions. Mechanical sensors within the mouse detect the direction the ball is rolling and move the screen pointer accordingly.

Mice (or mouses) contain at least one button and sometimes as many as three, which have different functions depending on what program is running. Some mice also include a *scroll wheel* for scrolling through long documents.

An *optomechanical* mouse is the same as a mechanical mouse but uses optical sensors to detect the motion of the ball. An *optical* mouse uses a laser to detect the mouse's movement.

Index

F

Q

R

S

CPSIA information can be obtained at www.ICGtesting.com
Printed in the USA
BVOW021128130312

284854BV00006B/1/P